Sacred
Symbols

Sacred Symbols

A Visual Tour of World Faith

Edited by Robert Adkinson

Abrams, New York

Library of Congress Control Number: 2008938283
ISBN 978-0-8109-3796-3

Printed and bound in China
10 9 8 7 6 5 4 3 2 1

Abrams books are available at special discounts when
purchased in quantity for premiums and promotions as
well as fundraising or educational use. Special editions
can also be created to specification. For details, contact
specialmarkets@hnabooks.com or the address below.

HNA
harry n. abrams, inc.
a subsidiary of La Martinière Groupe

115 West 18th Street
New York, NY 10011
www.hnabooks.com

CONTENTS

INTRODUCTION

The sacred symbols of ancient tradition take us to the very heart of what it is to be human. Even in contemporary Western culture, seemingly dominated by rationalism, consumerism, and constant visual novelty, shared symbols continue to shape our mental and emotional landscapes. The urge to articulate the interconnections of the universe and our place within it is an intrinsic human need that we share with our very earliest ancestors.

This book represents a visual compendium of the timeless efforts of human beings to explain and contain the universe around them. It brings together some of the world's most potent sacred signs and images under three categories – peoples, religions and mysteries. Within these broad themes, the range is immense. It encompasses traditions both Eastern and Western, ancient and living, and draws upon art, ritual, myth and spirituality. Each tradition explored is fascinating in its own right; surveyed together they reveal many of the most fundamental archetypes of the human experience.

At the dawn of history, the whole world – animate and inanimate, natural and supernatural – was interpreted symbolically.

Life, death and rebirth were in constant close proximity, and these unceasing transformations were explained through stories and symbols: the passage between this world and the next, the rebirth of each new day and each spring. Such stories were symbolically relived through ritual, art, dance, sacrifice, masks, hieroglyphs, talismans, fetishes, architecture and music. They served to keep a community in close connection with its defining narratives, above all its creation myths and stories of origin.

The ancient Egyptians employed symbols to represent the forces of the universe and all it contained: the gods and man, the creation and the afterlife, the struggle between good and evil, life and death. Even their written language was to a degree symbolic. The Celts saw all the elements of the natural world as possessed with individual spirits. So too did many of the native peoples of the Americas, for whom the landscape was animated by a multiplicity of spiritual presences that were venerated and placated through symbol, myth and art in the context of an often heroic struggle for survival. The Maya lived in a world dense with multi-layered meaning. In Maya iconography, a house, a maize field, a great caiman or even a tortoise could represent the earth. Natural and supernatural phenomena were in constant interaction in a choreographed cosmic ritual.

The world's religions have always communicated their belief systems through symbol, both to convey the power of the universe and to express its deeper, more mysterious truths. In Buddhism, lacking an all-powerful creator deity, many of the complex principles of the faith are articulated through art and architecture, and through accounts of the life of the Buddha himself. Buddhist art is rich with symbol and symbolic gesture, whether the Buddha is depicted with hands folded in meditation, reaching his right hand to earth to indicate enlightenment, or seated under a parasol, symbol of the fig tree that sheltered him as he attained nirvana. Such a language of symbol is remarkably resonant in conveying the non-dogmatic teachings of this inclusive and tolerant faith.

The Taoist tradition is similarly devoid of an all-powerful god; indeed it is neither a formal religion nor even a structured philosophy. Yet its rich iconography is laden with meaning, evolved through hundreds of years of Chinese art. With its emphasis on the harmonious interplay of opposing elements in the universe – *yin* and *yang*, male and female, life and death, light and dark, ebb and flow, earth and heaven – the Taoist worldview is one that touches a deeply intuitive chord.

Representing a more structured belief system than either Buddhism or Taoism, Christianity is no less replete with potent symbolism. In the Christian tradition, the suffering and martyrdom of Jesus Christ came to symbolize all human suffering. The lamb of God, the dove of the Holy Spirit, the bread and wine of the Last Supper, the attributes of the saints: such emblems acquired a deep resonance as they were reiterated through ritual, liturgy and art over the course of two millennia.

Other bodies of symbolism transcend ethnic, historical and religious boundaries. The mandala, timeless and strangely all-embracing, is one of the great symbols of human experience. Jung considered it one of the archetypes of the collective unconscious, and a therapeutic device for helping to restore the shattered psyche. Its concentric structure is both cosmic and microcosmic – suggestive of the physical form of the universe as well as the individual soul's journey through a succession of interior states to the centre of all understanding, the point of supreme consciousness. The mandala has parallels across multiple cultures, far beyond its Hindu and Buddhist homelands, where it is revered as a focus for meditation and a symbol of the unity of all phenomena and experience.

Truly universal is the sexual experience, symbolic across numerous different cultures not only of procreation and fertility but of the confluence of elemental forces shaping and driving the universe. Mother Earth and Father Sky, *yin* earth and *yang* heavens: the sexual principle is repeatedly represented as the energizing force in the cosmic cycle of birth, death, rebirth and renewal.

The book concludes with an investigation of the complex and enigmatic symbolism of the Tarot, which has defied rational explanation since its first appearance in the 15th century. With its links to the occult and divination, this mysterious body of imagery retains a powerful hold on the imagination.

The enduring bodies of symbols explored throughout this book represent an extraordinary diversity of cultures and traditions. Together they reveal not so much the differences from one set of beliefs to the next, but rather the shared instinct to express the fundamental truths of the human experience through the power of creativity.

Peoples

Ancient Egypt

A WORLD OF SYMBOLS

For the ancient Egyptians the whole world, as they saw it, was represented symbolically. From the sun and the Nile, which gave them food and sustenance, to the animal kingdom, wild and domestic, everything was imbued with hidden meaning. Even their architecture, and especially

that associated with funerary rites, was full of complex meaning and significance. At its deepest level, symbolism was the means by which the Egyptians expressed their speculations about the nature of life itself – the creation, the afterlife and the struggle between good and evil.

Page 14 and above Examples of painted hieroglyphs and symbols from ancient Egypt.

Chronological table

Late Predynastic Period (*c.* 3000 BC)

Early Dynastic Period (2950–2650 BC)
Dynasty 1	2950–2750 BC
Dynasty 2	2750–2650 BC

Old Kingdom (2650–2175 BC)
Dynasty 3	2650–2575 BC
Dynasty 4	2575–2450 BC
Dynasty 5	2450–2325 BC
Dynasty 6	2325–2175 BC

First Intermediate Period (2175–1975 BC)
Dynasties 7–8	2175–2125 BC
Dynasties 9–10	2125–1975 BC

Middle Kingdom (2080–1755 BC)
Dynasty 11	2080–1940 BC
Dynasty 12	1938–1755 BC

Second Intermediate Period (1755–1539 BC)
Dynasty 13	1755–1630 BC
Dynasties 14–17	1630–1539 BC

# of ancient Egypt

New Kingdom (1539–1069 BC)

Dynasty 18	1539–1292 BC
Dynasty 19	1292–1190 BC
Dynasty 20	1190–1069 BC

Third Intermediate Period (1069–657 BC)

Dynasty 21	1069–945 BC
Dynasty 22	945–715 BC
Dynasty 23	830–715 BC
Dynasty 24	730–715 BC
Dynasty 25	800–657 BC (Kushite)

Late Period (664–332 BC)

Dynasty 26	664–525 BC (Saite)
Dynasty 27	525–404 BC (Persian)
Dynasty 28	404–399 BC
Dynasty 29	399–380 BC
Dynasty 30	380–343 BC
Dynasty 31	343–332 BC (Persian)

Greco-Roman Period (332 BC–AD 395)

Ptolemaic Dynasty	332–30 BC
Roman emperors	30 BC–AD 395

A gift from the gods

the written language of the ancient Egyptians was truly symbolic and very much associated with the gods themselves. Just how closely the image and the act of writing itself were connected is demonstrated by there being a single word for 'drawing' and 'writing'. In hieroglyphic writing, the gods were signified by their symbols; Horus was represented by a falcon, Isis by a throne, Seth by a desert animal with an arrow-like tail and Anubis by a jackal. And much of the rest of the language was symbolic : 'to walk' was signified by two legs; 'house'

was represented by a rectangle with an opening in its lower part.

The representations of the god Thoth were many – as an ibis-headed deity, baboon, or god of the moon. Of great importance to the Egyptians was his role as god of writing and patron of scribes, since language was believed to be a gift direct from the gods. The god-baboon Thoth is often represented watching over a crouching, subservient scribe.

Opposite Detail of hieroglyphics found in the tomb of Queen Nefertari, near Luxor, Egypt.

Left A statuette of the god Thoth depicted with an ibis head.

CHAOS AND COSMOS

Symbols and gods of creation and the life force

The ancient Egyptian religious texts offer several explanations of the creation, usually differing according to their place of origin. One strong tradition told of the emergence of a mound from the watery chaos. Another version of this tradition included a lotus floating upon the primeval waters and then opening to reveal the new-born sun. Creation by utterance was another common tradition; at Memphis the creator god Ptah is supposed to have initiated the cosmos by simply speaking the thought.

Nut

Called 'the female pig who eats her piglets', mother of all the heavenly bodies which entered her mouth and emerged again from her womb, the sky goddess Nut is represented *(overleaf)* arching over Shu, her father, god of air, who helps to support her, and Geb, her husband and brother, god of the earth. As the goddess of the cyclical working of the cosmos, Nut was also intimately connected to the idea of resurrection. The sarcophagus and tomb chamber were often decorated with stars and the goddess's image.

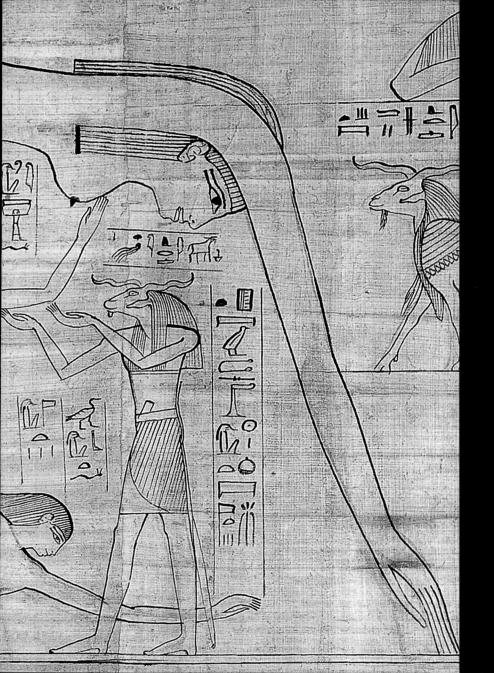

The sky goddess Nut, shown in a papyrus of the Twenty-first Dynasty.

Tefnut

One of the oldest Egyptian creation myths visualized the earth as a mound rising from the watery chaos of Nun. On the mound was the self-created Atum, who then created Shu, god of air, and Tefnut, goddess of moisture, thus releasing duality into the world and the beginning of the sexual cycle. Atum was eventually assimilated into Re, the sun god, making Tefnut the daughter of the sun. In this papyrus *(opposite)* of the Nineteenth Dynasty, Tefnut is represented with an *ankh* symbol in the role of one of the judges of the Underworld. She is depicted with a ram's head although often she had the head of a lion.

Opposite Tefnut, goddess of life-giving dew, Papyrus of Hunefer, Nineteenth Dynasty.

Apis bull

as one of the strongest procreative symbols of ancient Egypt, the bull could represent the composite god of creation, the primeval waters or even the inundation of the Nile. This identification with the creative life force also meant that the bull was identified with the Egyptian king and a number of New Kingdom monarchs were described as 'mighty bull' or 'bull of Horus'.

Opposite Twentieth-Dynasty coffin painting showing the bull as god of creation and rebirth.

Right Bronze sculpture of Apis bull, Late Period.

Hail to you, you who shine in your disc, a living soul who goes up from the horizon…
I know the names of the seven cows and their bull, who give bread and beer, who are beneficial to souls.

The Egyptian Book of the Dead, Spell 148

༠ Sun and moon ☽

The passage of the sun through the vault of the heavens is represented by the sky goddess Nut; she touches the western and eastern horizons with her hands and feet. Nut was the deity for all heavenly bodies and mother of the sun god Re, who was swallowed by his mother in the evening when the sun set, and then reborn in the morning. Nut was thus a symbol of resurrection and rebirth. In Heliopolitan theology she was the daughter of Shu, the air god, and sister of Geb, the earth god. The moon was the 'sun shining at night', the left eye of the sky god, known as the Eye of Horus. It was usually represented in the form of a disc resting on a crescent, worn as a headdress by the moon god Khons.

Opposite A tomb-ceiling painting of the sun's night-time journey through the body of Nut, Twentieth Dynasty.

Left Bronze statuette of Iah, 'the moon' in human form, crowned by the Eye of Horus, Late Period.

A limestone carving of the royal family, Eighteenth Dynasty.

O sun disc, Lord of the sunbeams, who shines forth from the horizon every day: may you shine in the face of the deceased, for he worships you in the morning, he propitiates you in the evening. May he moor in the night barque, may he mix with the unwearying stars in the sky.

The Egyptian Book of the Dead, Spell 15

Opposite A mummy receiving the life-giving rays, Twenty-sixth Dynasty.

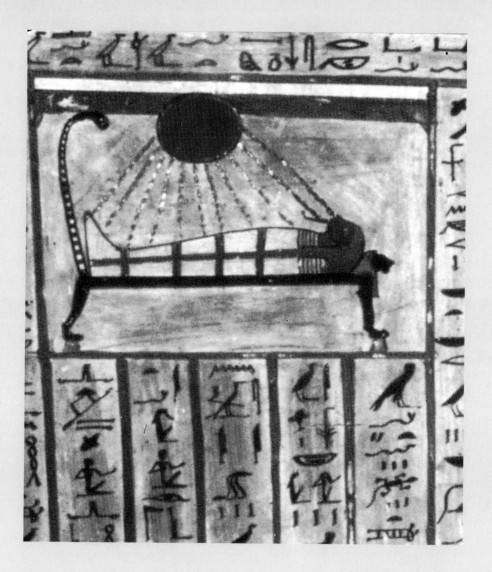

Osiris

'The eternally good king' or 'the perfect one' under his received name of Wennefer, Osiris was at the centre of the most extensive symbolism of ancient Egypt. He began as a fertility god with a special association with corn and with the life-giving waters of the Nile, called the 'efflux of Osiris'. After receiving the rulership of the earth from his father Geb, Osiris introduced viticulture and agriculture to the country. All this inspired the envy of his brother Seth, who caused him to be drowned in the Nile, symbolizing the flooding of the land and the new harvest. After death the god was thought to have been dismembered, although this myth may only have arisen because so many places claimed his remains.

Hail to you, Osiris Wennefer, the vindicated, the son of Nut; king in the Thinite nome; foremost of the westerners; Lord of Abydos; Lord of Power, greatly majestic.

The Egyptian Book of the Dead, Spell 128

Opposite In a painting from his burial tomb, Tutankhamun – represented as Osiris – undergoes the ritual of the opening of the mouth, meant to re-animate the deceased.

Osiris and Horus

Divine mourners, and sister goddesses, Isis and Nephthys
protect the *djed* pillar, symbol of Osiris, with their wings.

the falcon, king of the air, was the creature of Horus and symbol of divine kingship. Here, this expression of domination and triumph surmounts the *djed* pillar, ancient fetish and feature of rustic fertility rites. Given its architectural character, the pillar took on associations of stability and, most interesting, became a symbol for Osiris at the beginning of the New Kingdom, when it was seen to represent the god's backbone. The raising of the pillar represented the victory of Osiris over Seth.

Right Djed pillar surmounted by the falcon with the sun disc.

Maat

Without this goddess, the whole process
of creation and constant renewal would have
been meaningless. She symbolized the laws of
existence – law, truth and the world order – and
judges were thought of as the priests of Maat.
The cyclical nature of life would have been
impossible without her: she was food and
drink to Re, her father, the sun god. She
was represented wearing an ostrich feather,
which came to be a symbol of truth.

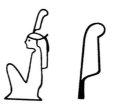

Opposite Maat with
an ostrich feather,
symbol of truth, in
her headband.

The tree of life

The tree, especially the date palm and sycamore, was indeed the symbol of life for the ancient Egyptians, since it grew where there was life-giving water. Sycamores had particular significance, and two special ones were supposed to stand at the eastern gate of heaven from which Re emerged each day. There was widespread worship of the tree in the Nile Valley and several deities were believed to have been born from trees – Horus from the acacia, Re from the sycamore and Wepwawet from the tamarisk. Images of female tree spirits, representing the sky goddesses Nut and Hathor, abound; the deities gave water and fruit to the soul of the deceased, which was represented in bird form.

SPELL FOR KNOWING THE SOUL OF EASTERNERS

I know those two trees of turquoise between which Re goes forth, which have grown up at the supports of Shu at that gate of the Lord of East where Re goes forth.

The Egyptian Book of the Dead, Spell 109

Opposite The goddess Isis from a tomb painting of Thutmosis III.

The waters of life

It is hardly surprising that water in ancient Egypt was the subject of extensive symbolism; it was, after all, the very life source of the country. It was the primeval matter from which all things had come, it provided purification and it was a symbol of reproduction. As god of vegetation, Osiris was also lord of the waters of the Nile. He was responsible for the river's annual inundation of the surrounding plane, which was vital to the cultivation and fertility of the land, separately represented by Isis.

Opposite The deceased drinking water in the realm of the dead, Twentieth Dynasty.

SPELL FOR DRINKING WATER IN THE REALM OF THE DEAD

May the great water be opened for Osiris, may the cool water of Thoth and the water of Hapi be thrown open for the Lord of the Horizon in this my name of Pedsu. May I be granted power over the waters like the limbs of Seth, for I am he who crosses the sky, I am the Lion of Re, I am the Slayer who eats the foreleg, the leg of beef is extended to me, the pools of the Field of Rushes serve me, limitless eternity is given to me, for I am he who inherited eternity, to whom everlasting life was given.

The Egyptian Book of the Dead, Spell 62

The river of life

The Nile, personified here as a man, bears the palm rib, which is also the hieroglyph for 'year', symbolizing the annual flooding of the river *(opposite)*. Although fish were generally thought unclean, the bulti fish was taken as a potent symbol of rebirth, a reference to the incubation and hatching of eggs in its mouth *(below)*.

The power and standing of gods and kings was expressed through an elaborate system of personal symbols, from headdress to amulet. The greatest symbolic embodiment of regal power was the Sphinx, firm but benevolent.

POWER AND POTENCY

Symbols of status and good fortune

Sphinx and pyramid,
two of the strongest
symbols of status
and power in ancient
Egyptian thought.

The life force

the creative force and power of life found expression at the personal, individual level in the *ka*. Symbolized by two upraised arms, the *ka* was a person's double, embodying intellectual and spiritual power. The defensive posture of the arms is designed to ward off evil forces, which may attack the life spirit of the wearer. Each person was born with his or her *ka*, which was a constant companion through life and lived on after death, returning to its divine origin. However, the *ka* did need sustenance, and food itself was regarded as having its own *ka*. In its earliest form the *ka* represented male potency and only later came to have its all-embracing significance.

Opposite King Hor
wearing a headdress
in the shape of the
ka hieroglyph,
Thirteenth Dynasty.

Crown

the crown of the Egyptian king was looked upon as a source of nourishment whereby its power was transferred to the ruler. Since Egypt was a country of two lands the kings wore the 'Double Crown', the *pschent*, combining the symbolic flowering lotus of the White Crown of Upper Egypt with the papyrus plant, which represented the Red Crown of Lower Egypt. According to the period the crowns took different forms, from the 'double feathers' crown of two upright ostrich plumes to the *khepresh* or Blue Crown with gold ornamentation. The royal crowns were also seen as the eye of the sun god or as a flame around the king.

Opposite Tutankhamun in the form of Osiris, wearing a gold headdress with a vulture and cobra.

Headdress

The close association of Egyptian deities and animals was constantly expressed in the animal-headed figures in Egyptian art. Power is conferred by the headdress and its form indicates the status of the wearer. A symbol of evil among the dwellers of the Nile Delta was Seth, a human figure with a headdress of an indeterminate species, part antelope, part anteater.

Above Statuette of the god Amun, with ram's horns and double crown, Twenty-second Dynasty.

'He whose hinder parts are extended' is the name of the keeper of the second gate; 'Shifting of face' is the name of him who guards it; 'Burner' is the name of him who makes report in it.

The Egyptian Book of the Dead, Spell 144

Opposite Animal-headed figures in a tomb painting of the second gate of the Underworld.

Vulture headdress

When the Egyptian king went into battle he was protected by a vulture with a white headdress. His own head cloth was a symbol of the Upper Egyptian national goddess Nekhbet, who was also characterized by her wearing of a vulture headdress. The vulture was, surprisingly, thought to play a protective role in the land of the dead. In the Late Period the bird came to embody the female principle, as opposed to the beetle, which was the embodiment of the male principle. As the heraldic animal of Upper Egypt and of the goddess Nekhbet, the vulture became an especially potent royal symbol and was often represented in royal graves. It was also the sacred animal of the goddess Mut, worshipped at Thebes.

Opposite Queen Nefertari wearing the vulture headdress, symbol of protection.

Ankh

The original significance of this mysterious Egyptian symbol is not clear. It has been suggested that its shape has sexual connotations, although there is support for the theory that it represents a simple sandal strap. Symbol of life and irresistible strength, representative of the life-giving attributes of air and water, the *ankh* was given by the gods to the king and is usually shown in the hands of a deity or its associated animal. This was one of the most powerful of all Egyptian amulets and retained its influence throughout ancient Egyptian history, eventually entering Christian iconography during the Coptic period.

Opposite The goddess Hathor with the *ankh* in the form of Osiris, Thebes, Twentieth Dynasty.

Above A gilded wooden mirror box in the *ankh* form.

Shen ring

the perfection of the *shen* ring amulet, without beginning or end, made it a very obvious symbol of eternity. Its round form also associated it with the disc of the sun, and it was often depicted being held by animals and birds, such as the falcon, with strong solar connections. 'Magic' rings were very popular and were believed to give protection from various illnesses.

SPELL FOR A KNOT AMULET OF RED JASPER

You have your blood, O Isis; you have your power, O Isis; you have your magic, O Isis. The amulet is a protection for this Great One which will drive away whoever would commit a crime against him.

The Egyptian Book of the Dead, Spell 156

Opposite The goddess Isis, hands stretched over a *shen* ring, symbolizing eternity, Eighteenth Dynasty.

Eyes watch over a falcon-headed god,
forming a protective shield.

The eyes of Horus

The right eye of the falcon god Horus was known as the 'Eye of Re', the eye of the sun god; the left eye, the 'Eye of Horus', was regarded as the symbol of the moon. Of Horus it was written, 'When he opens his eyes he fills the universe with light but when he shuts them darkness comes into being.' The sacred eye symbol was undoubtedly a sign of protection; it appeared in countless articles of jewelry, especially amulets, and two eyes were often painted on the left side of coffins to enable the deceased to see the way ahead.

SPELL FOR BRINGING A SACRED EYE BY THE DECEASED

Thoth has fetched the Sacred Eye, having pacified the eye after Re had sent it away. It was very angry, but Thoth pacified it from anger after it had been far away. If I be hale, it will be hale, and the deceased will be hale.

The Egyptian Book of the Dead, Spell 167

BESTIARY AND BELIEF

Symbols from nature

The natural world and its parts – animals, birds, flowers – were seen by the ancient Egyptians to symbolize much greater natural phenomena. The scarab rolling its ball of dung was the sun god rolling the sun's orb across the sky. In one version of the cosmos, the wings of a falcon were seen as the broad sweep of the heavens, the speckled underside of the feathers representing the sky above.

Opposite A sa-ta snake walking on human legs, a symbol of mystery and life creation.

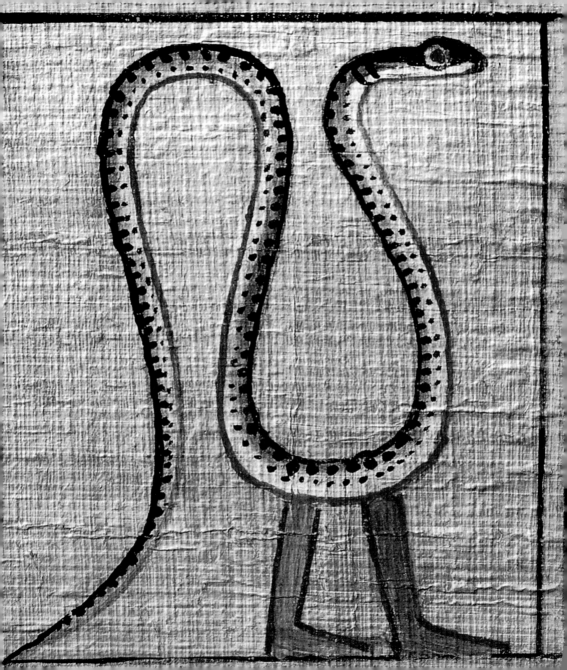

Baboon

Above Faïence figure of a baboon clutching the eye symbol.

Opposite Funerary decoration depicting baboons worshipping the birth of the sun.

Closely associated with Thoth, the god of writing, the baboon is often represented in Egyptian art in the same context as scribes. Such figures often bear the lunar crescent and the solar disc on their heads: Thoth had originally been a moon god and it was believed that the cries uttered by baboons in the morning were a welcome to the early sun. The chief cult centre of Thoth was at Hermopolis, where the god assumed the form of the baboon after merging with a deity of the region.

I am Thoth the skilled scribe whose hands are pure, a possessor of purity, who drives away evil, who writes what is true, who detests falsehood, whose pen defends the Lord of All; master of laws, who interprets writings, whose words establish the Two Lands.

The Egyptian Book of the Dead, Spell 182

Cat

the image of the cat in the earliest Egyptian symbolism was probably derived from the jungle cat, which lived in the Nile Delta. In the New Kingdom the male cat was seen as an incarnation of the sun god and the she-cat as the solar eye. The domestic cat was the sacred animal of the goddess Bastet, usually depicted as a woman with the head of a cat.

Left A bronze figure of a cat, representing the goddess Bastet, Late Period.

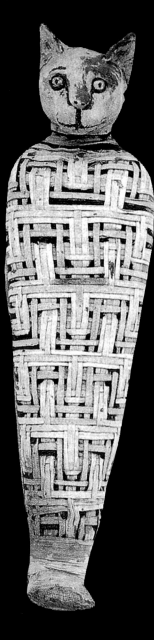

Cats sacred to the
goddess Bastet were
mummified when
they died.

Scarab

Detail of a scarab bracelet from the tomb of Tutankhamun, Thebes.

Symbol of self-creation, the scarab was believed to come directly into being from the balls of animal dung that it used to protect its eggs and larva. It was associated with the sun and therefore with life-giving warmth and light, and pottery models of the scarab were often placed in tombs as a symbol of the renewal of life. In its solar role, the scarab represented the morning sun in its god form of Khepri. In his beetle form, the god rose as the morning sun from the eastern horizon. A strong life god, Khepri also symbolized resurrection.

I have flown up like the primeval ones, I have become Khepri, I have grown as a plant, I have clad myself as a tortoise, I am the essence of every god.

The Egyptian Book of the Dead, Spell 83

Falcon

Gold falcon ornament clutching shen rings and ankhs.

So many Egyptian deities were associated with the falcon that the image of the bird came to be virtually synonymous with 'god'. Its regal flight and aggressive qualities made it a natural symbol for Horus, king of the gods, and for divine kingship in general. Other falcon gods included Month, the god of war, Re, the sun god, and Sokar, the god of mortuaries. The original image of Horus was of a falcon protecting the heavens and earth with outstretched wings.

Right Bronze figure of the falcon god Horus, Twenty-sixth Dynasty.

Ibis

the sacred ibis enjoyed very special status as the incarnation of Thoth, lord of the moon and the protector of scribes. Thoth's main cult centre at Hermopolis was also the burial ground for thousands of mummified ibises. The crested ibis was also used as a symbol for transfiguration.

Opposite In Spell 183 of *The Egyptian Book of the Dead* Thoth, with an ibis head, offers symbols, including the *ankh*, to Osiris for 'all life and dominion'.

Right Ibis coffin in gilded wood, silver and gold, Greco-Roman Period.

Vulture

Armlet of Queen Ahhotpe in the form of the vulture goddess Nekhbet.

Cobra

The cobra was seen principally as a solar symbol, with close connections to many deities. One of the most notable was the goddess Wadjet of the city of Buto and, through her, the cobra came to be an emblem of Lower Egypt.

SPELL FOR BEING TRANSFORMED INTO A SNAKE

I am a long-lived snake; I pass the night and am reborn every day. I am a snake which is in the limits of the earth; I pass the night and am reborn, renewed and rejuvenated every day.

The Egyptian Book of the Dead, Spell 87

Rising cobra wearing the Red Crown of Lower Egypt, made from sheet gold, Late Period.

Crocodile

The crocodile was seen as an agent of disorder and was associated with the evil god Seth. So strong was crocodile imagery in Egyptian symbolic thought that *The Egyptian Book of the Dead* contains a

In this papyrus of the Twenty-first Dynasty, a priestess drinks river water while faced with a crocodile representing the god Geb.

Get back you crocodile of the East who lives on those who are mutilated.
Detestation of you is in my belly, and I have gone away, for I am Osiris.

The Egyptian Book of the Dead, Spell 32

number of recipes for repelling the reptiles. Yet, since it had emerged
from the waters like the sun god, the crocodile also had more positive
connotations as a force for life and renewal.

SPELL FOR BEING TRANSFORMED INTO A LOTUS

I am this pure lotus which went forth from the sunshine, which is at the nose of Re; I have descended so that I may seek it for Horus, for I am the pure one who issued from the fen.

The Egyptian Book of the Dead, Spell 81A

Lotus

as the sun rises in the morning in the East, the water lily, the lotus, opens itself to greet the renewal of light. So the flower became the symbol of the sun re-emerging after the night and therefore associated with the sun god Re who is portrayed in *The Egyptian Book of the Dead* as a golden youth rising from the lotus. Thus the flower, especially the blue lotus, also came to symbolize rebirth. The portrait head of Tutankhamun *(opposite)* is shown rising from a blue lotus, signifying his resurrection, while lotus inlays *(below)* were a common decorative motif in burial tombs.

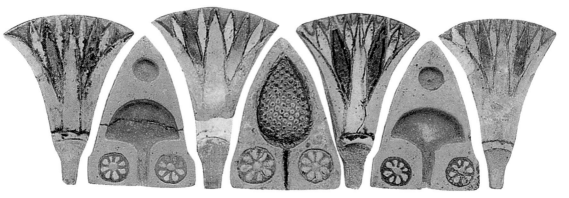

THE AFTERLIFE

Symbols for the dead

The great pyramids
of Giza, Fourth
Dynasty.

Ancient Egyptian architecture – especially shrines and burial places – had symbolic meaning. The pyramid, which may also have symbolized the mound of creation rising from the primeval waters, was intimately associated with the sun.

Anubis

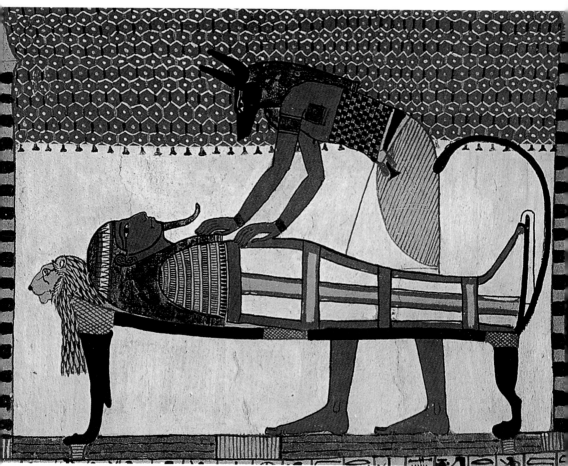

Anubis embalms the nobleman Sennedjem, Nineteenth Dynasty.

Usually represented in canine form – dog or jackal – Anubis was the principal god of the dead before Osiris. He was closely associated with the necropolis and known as 'God of the Hallowed Land'. Representations of Anubis were placed in the tomb to guard the mummification chamber and frighten away evil.

SPELL FOR BREATHING AIR AND HAVING POWER
OVER WATER IN THE REALM OF THE DEAD

I shall cross to the mansion of him who finds faces; 'Collector of Souls' is the name of the ferryman...you shall give me a jug of milk, a *shens* loaf, a *persen* loaf, a jug of beer and a portion of meat in the mansions of Anubis.

The Egyptian Book of the Dead, Spell 58

Right Wood figure of Anubis, god of the dead, coated with painted stucco, Late Period.

Doors and stairs

the symbolism of the door was dual – it could represent closure or entry and is seen with both such meanings in ancient Egyptian art. In tombs and shrines, doors would be decorated with various symbols, usually signifying the transition from one state to the next – into heaven or into the deepest part of the Underworld. Tomb doors depicted as open signified that the spirit of the deceased, symbolically, had free access to the buried body and that the *ka* could come and go at will.

As symbols of transition, ascension and descent, staircases and ladders were as potent as doorways. Every Egyptian tomb incorporated a stairway, which led down into the inner chamber.

Opposite Interior of the chapel of a nobleman, Sixth Dynasty.

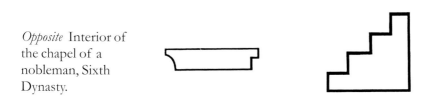

Shrine

In its Upper Egyptian form, the *per-wer* or *kar*, the shrine, came to symbolize the whole of the southern region. Such shrines housed the image of the appropriate god and were usually kept in a separate room at the rear of the god's house, from which it might be taken for religious processions or rituals. The Lower Egyptian shrine, the *per-nu*, had a domed roof and high side-posts, in contrast to the sloping roof and prominent cornice of the *per-wer*. In *The Book of Gates* – a text included in burial tombs to help the deceased navigate through the Underworld – a row of twelve *per-nu* shrines is shown with doors open displaying the gods inside, while a huge serpent lies along the whole length as a symbol of protection.

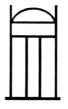

Opposite Shrine from the tomb of Tutankhamun in the Upper Egyptian *per-wer* form, Eighteenth Dynasty.

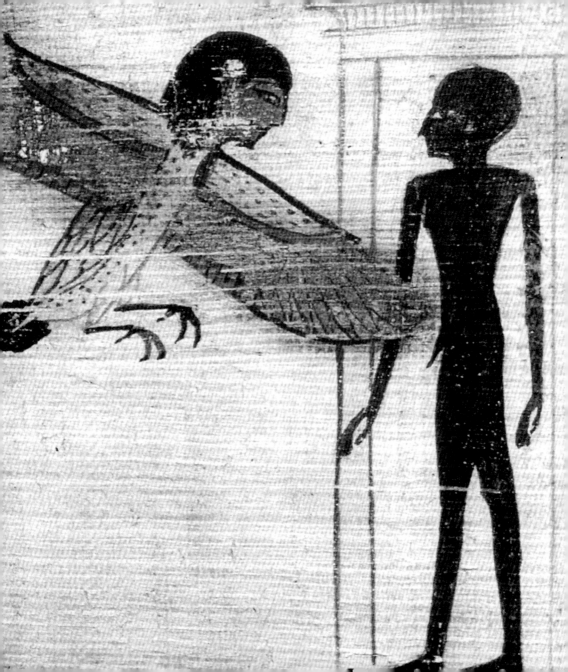

Ba

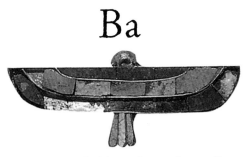

A human-headed *ba* in glass and cornelian.

Often inadequately translated as 'soul', the word *ba* should really be more properly thought of as referring to a psychic force. First ascribed to gods, then later applied to all people, the *ba* was the spiritual aspect of the human being, which survived death.

SPELL FOR GOING TO AND FRO IN THE REALM OF THE DEAD

O you who cause the perfected souls to draw to the house of Osiris, may you cause the excellent soul of the deceased to draw near with you to the house of Osiris. May he hear as you hear, may he see as you see, may he stand as you stand, may he sit as you sit.

The Egyptian Book of the Dead, Spell 1

Opposite The *ba* was often shown in bird form in tomb paintings.

The Celts

For many people the term 'Celtic' conjures up the culture and mythology of the western extremes of Europe – lands steeped in hero cults and Arthurian romance. This was the view of the Celts promoted by the so-called 'Celtic Revival' of the 19th century. But history is more complex: Classical commentators described as 'Celt' a large group of peoples living initially north of the Alps and then spreading eastwards and southwards. During the

thousand years that elapsed before the conversion of the western Celts to Christianity, this warlike people developed a way of life that was highly informed by religious cults and their associated symbolism. For the Celts everything in the natural world possessed its own spirit. With the arrival of Christianity, many pagan Celtic deities merged easily with the characters of the new religion.

Page 90 Bronze figure, Bouray, France, 1st century BC – 1st century AD.

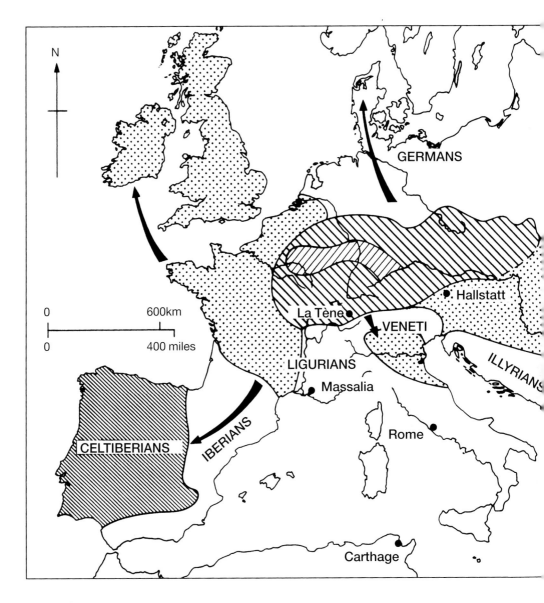

N

0 ___ 600km
0 ___ 400 miles

GERMANS

Hallstatt

La Tène

VENETI

LIGURIANS

ILLYRIANS

Massalia

CELTIBERIANS

IBERIANS

Rome

Carthage

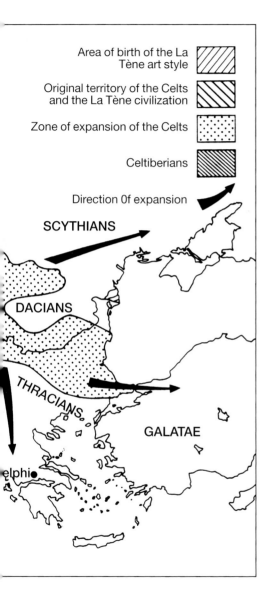

Area of birth of the La Tène art style

Original territory of the Celts and the La Tène civilization

Zone of expansion of the Celts

Celtiberians

Direction 0f expansion

SCYTHIANS

DACIANS

THRACIANS

GALATAE

elphi●

Left Regions of Europe occupied by the Celts from the 5th century BC to the Roman conquests of the 1st century AD.

THE SACRED

Many of the focal points for Celtic religious ritual and symbolism were natural sites. Votive offerings have been discovered in lakes, rivers and marshes, and near springs. Hill regions were often the home for cults devoted to the worship of mountain gods. Such places, which also included sacred groves and forest clearings, might be marked by small shrines or, even more characteristically, by phallic standing stones.

The Ring of Brodgar in Orkney, Scotland
was originally made of 60 standing stones.

LANDSCAPE

These were used to delimit sacred places throughout the Celtic world and may very well have originated in attempts to imitate the sacred tree. In the sacred landscape of pre-Celtic Britain, too, sites with standing stones were clearly designated as places for religious activity. In the early Christian era, holy men in Ireland and Scotland continued to seek out desolate places in order to experience the concentration of great natural forces.

Standing stones

throughout the Celtic lands, from Ireland in the west to central Europe, sacred places were often marked by the erection of a wooden or stone pillar. As an expression of vital energy, the form probably derived from a desire to imitate the tree, an especially potent symbol for the Celts. Undoubtedly, too, several such stones were meant to express the brute, primal force associated with the phallus. They could also serve as landmarks in the often desolate areas in which they are commonly found. Sometimes they were elaborately worked and carved, as in the Iron Age Turoe stone *(opposite)* in County Galway, Ireland, with curvilinear motifs typical of Celtic decoration.

The sacred site of Tara

The royal and sacred hill of Tara *(opposite)* in County Meath, Ireland, was a symbol of great significance for the Irish Celts from late Neolithic times to the Christian era. Originally fortified during the Iron Age, the hill became the seat of the kings of Ireland. The site is notable for its two joined ring forts, in one of which stands the Lia Fáil, known as the 'Stone of Destiny', which was said to cry out aloud if touched by the rightful king-elect.

According to traditional accounts in Irish mythology, no mortal king could assume true sovereignty at Tara without first coupling with one of the goddesses of the land. The great goddess-queen of Connacht, Medb, is said to have cohabited with nine kings.

Mountain goddess

 In County Kerry, Ireland, stand two rounded hills *(opposite)* known as Dá Chich Anann, or the breasts of Anu, a mother goddess of the Irish Celts. The fundamental animism of the pagan Celts meant that many cults grew up which attached themselves to specific natural phenomena. Mountains and high places in particular were important locations for religious activity. Another mountain god was a Celtic form of Jupiter, worshipped especially in the Pyrenees.

The Celtic mythology of Ireland is rich in traditional tales of magic and taboo, mainly because the country never underwent Romanization. Anu, frequently confused in legend with Danu or Dana, was a fertility goddess, mother of the Tuatha Dé Danann ('People of the goddess Danu'), the last generation of gods to have ruled the earth.

The well-springs of life

Water, in all its manifestations, fascinated the Celts. A whole universe of myth, ritual and symbolism surrounds seas, lakes, rivers, springs, wells and marshland. Throughout Celtic Europe, from the Bronze Age onwards, votive offerings of fine goods and jewelry, weapons and even human and animal sacrifices were made to lakes, rivers and bogs. The apparently spontaneous movement of water, especially when rising from the ground, must have seemed evidence of supernatural forces at work, and curative shrines grew up around important springs and wells. Water from the earth may also have been looked on as a form of contact with the Otherworld.

The Romano-Celtic period saw a large number of cults associated with water gods grow up: a Celtic Neptune at Bath *(above)* and water goddesses at High Rochester, Northumberland *(opposite)*, are examples of stonework devoted to water deities.

A contemporary drawing of the Celtic Tree of Life.

Trees of life and death

The veneration with which the Celts regarded the tree, either singly or in groups, is amply evident through the number of shrines devoted to it and its close association with the standing stone, the focal point of many sacred places. Trees could also reflect the joining of lower and upper worlds, their roots burrowing beneath the ground while their branches reached to the sky. The association of trees with hunting is beautifully illustrated in one scene on the Gundestrup Cauldron (see p. 111), found in a peat bog in Jutland, in which a procession is shown carrying a sacred tree, associating it with images of Cernunnos, the stag god. A more sinister and bloody association of trees is described by Tacitus: the Druids often used sacred groves as sites for human sacrifice.

METAMORPHOSES

Flux and change characterized Celtic life, customs and religious symbolism, perhaps a reflection of the migratory history of the people. Everything and everyone could be represented as something else; Irish and Welsh mythology is full of tales of animals who were once humans, and gods

OF GODS AND MEN

in both human and animal shape. This ambiguity extended to the representation of all human-like forms and functions in multi-headed figures, masks and headdresses. The final metamorphosis, death, sometimes ritually violent in the form of sacrifice, was regarded as a minor interruption to a long life, which would continue to flourish in the Otherworld.

A sculpture from Roquepertuse, France, depicting a Janus-headed warrior and war god.

War gods and warriors

In the cult of the warrior the subtle ambiguities of Celtic symbolism are very evident. Much of the iconography of fighting men is also a way of representing the gods, maintaining the continuity of human and divine. More strikingly, perhaps, the warriors are not all male, although the female ones also display the combination of aggression and sexual energy present in images of war gods, especially in Britain. A gold coin from Gaul *(opposite above)* depicts two horses side by side, one of which bears a triumphant horsewoman, naked apart from a belt and short cape. In Irish mythology the goddesses associated with war – Badb, Macha, Morrigan, Nemhain and Reb – were also fertility deities.

Opposite below Warriors, some with animal-crested helmets, bearing a sacred tree, from the Gundestrup Cauldron.

Although endowed with warlike associations and qualities, the Celtic female deities of the battlefield do not engage directly in combat themselves. Their function is to influence events, which may be achieved by metamorphosis. Morrigan, the Phantom Queen, appears to the Ulster warrior Cú Chulainn at various times in the guises of wolf, heifer and eel.

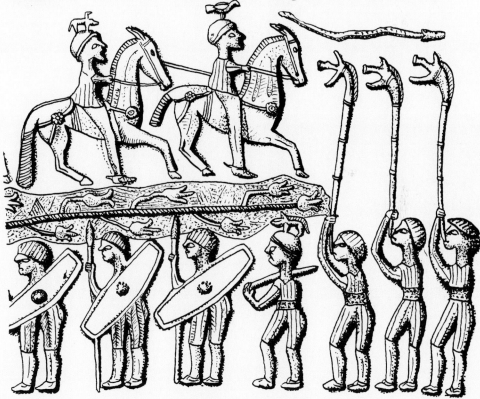

Bronze cult wagon of a warrior, 6th or 7th century BC.

Hunters and hunted

There was a very special relationship in Celtic mythology between the hunter and the hunted. The quarry, most notably the stag and the boar, was revered almost as much as the hunter deity. After all, the death of the beast led to its immortality, and there are many stories in the Celtic vernacular tradition of magical stags and boars luring their pursuers to death and the Otherworld. Other images and figures identify hunter gods and goddesses with the Classical Diana, especially in Gaul and Britain.

The deeds of Finn, the hero of the Fenian Cycle of Irish myths, and his hunter warriors, the Fianna, are largely ones of confrontation with the supernatural in the hunt. At the great hunt of the magic boar of Ben Balben in Sligo, Finn refused to give the healing water to Diarmaid, his rival in love, after the latter was wounded by the boar.

Mother goddesses

abundance and fecundity were central concerns of all ancient societies, and the Celts were no exception. The idea of an all-providing mother figure found constant expression throughout the Celtic lands in image and in legend. Often such goddesses were depicted in groups of three (the most sacred and potent number for the Celts) and surrounded by symbols of plenty – fruit, bread and corn; sometimes one of the three figures would be shown holding a baby. They were also closely associated with sacred sources, from small springs to great thermal baths, as at Aquae Sulis (present-day Bath), where they were known as the 'Suleviae'. The Irish goddesses of fertility were often identical with those of war, like Medb, who granted her favours to nine successive kings.

Opposite Triple mother-goddess sculpture, Vertault, France.

Phallus

if the triple goddess represented the female principle of fecundity, then the phallus was certainly the most potent symbol of the male principle. And like most other Celtic symbols it had both divine and human connotations. War gods were sometimes represented with erect phalli, which drew attention to their sexual potency and their association – like their female counterparts – with the fertility of the earth.

The famous chalk giant *(opposite)* of Cerne Abbas, Dorset, is shown brandishing a huge club, yet was almost certainly at the centre of local fertility rites. On another level of significance, this figure may also have represented Hercules.

On the Celtic festival of Beltane (1 May) the villagers of Cerne Abbas would dance around a maypole erected 20 metres (70 feet) further up the hill than the giant's head – a fertility ritual that was still practised into the early part of the 20th century.

Heads …

The severed head could also be a lethal weapon. Conchobar, mythical king of Ulster and first of the nine consorts of the goddess-queen Medb, was killed by a brain-ball (brains mixed with lime and then allowed to harden) made from the head of Meas Geaghra, king of Leinster.

... and head-hunters

One of the most shocking characteristics of the Celts for Classical commentators was that they were – at least in battle – head-hunters. The warrior who decapitated his enemy had more than proof of victory: he had also possessed himself of the sacred and protective powers supposed to reside within the human head. Skulls were frequently positioned at the doors of Celtic temples to act as spiritual guardians. Gods were depicted with over-large heads, while particular importance was attached to the double-faced janiform head, because of its ability to look in both directions at once. A famous example from Roquepertuse in the south of France shows the human and the divine, the warrior and the war god, gripped in the bill of a goose (*see pp. 108–9*).

Above Celtic coin depicting a head in profile.

Opposite Limestone head, 3rd or 2nd century BC, found in Bohemia.

The triple head

The number 'three' held deeply auspicious connotations for the Celts, certainly in Germany, Gaul and Britain. Of all the elements of Celtic iconography, it was the human head – symbol of spiritual potency – which was most often the subject of a triad. In traditional Celtic literature the presence and repetition of the number 'three' had the effect of strengthening and intensification. The mother goddess, for instance, was often represented in groups of three. But even in single-figure representations of gods or of their heads, it was not uncommon to find them given three faces – one main and two subsidiary.

Opposite Three-headed god on a terracotta vase, Bavay, France, 2nd century BC.

The transformed head

Masks and headdresses are often associated with the religious rituals and symbolism of the Celts. Although information about ceremonial is far from plentiful, archaeological evidence does seem to point to the wearing of special headgear during religious ceremonies. This could take the form of bronze diadems or chain headdresses to be worn over a leather helmet. Crowns were sometimes adorned with small reproductions of the human face, but relatively few full-scale masks have been found. These probably symbolized the metamorphosis of the priest into a superior being, and would have been held in front of the face during a procession to represent a deity.

Opposite A mask of a human face crowned with ram's horns forms the handle of a bronze flagon of the 5th century BC, discovered at Kleinaspergle, Germany.

There is a fascinating story of metamorphosis in *The Mabinogion,* a collection of ancient Welsh tales. Gwydion, a magician, provokes a war by sorcery between his uncle Math and Pryderi, the lord of Dyfed, so that his brother Gilfaethwy can seduce Math's virgin servant Goewin. On hearing of this deviousness, Math summons up his own magic, causing his two nephews to be turned into a stag and hind for one year, a boar and crow for the second, and male and female wolves for the third.

The divine beast

The interchangeability of deity, man and beast is a constant theme of Celtic iconography. Cernunnos, lord of the animals and of plenty, appears with the antlers of a stag; he is also closely associated with the snake, a symbol of renewal. Caer, the beloved of love god Oenghus, changes into swan form every alternate year.

Opposite A human-headed horse, detail from a bronze wine flagon, Reinheim, Germany, 5th–4th century BC.

The ultimate sacrifice

Most of the bloodier details of the sacrificial practices of the Celts come from Classical commentaries. Lucan refers to a sacred wood in the region of Marseilles, where every tree was smeared with the blood of victims. In Anglesey, according to Tacitus, there was a grove with altars covered with the grisly remains of druidical death ceremonies. Another favoured method of human sacrifice was the burning alive of the victim within a huge wicker cage – the 'wicker man'. Virtually all varieties of animal were sacrificed, although there does seem to have been a preference for boars, which were sometimes ritually buried alive. Yet sacrifice – the ultimate metamorphosis from life to death – was also the key to instant rebirth in the agelessness of the Otherworld.

Opposite One interpretation of this scene from the Gundestrup Cauldron is that the smaller figure is a sacrificial victim being pushed into a vat or cauldron.

SYMBOLIC

A lthough animal sacrifice was common in the Celtic world, both wild and domestic beasts were highly revered. And because Celtic religious belief was based very much upon the natural world, we find a great variety of animal representation: gods who are part beast, part human, and certain species that are clearly intended to be supernatural. Stags for

BEASTS

their virility, boars for their aggression, and horses
for their grace and strength, all seem to have been
particularly favoured symbols. Closer to domestic
life, the bull and dog were also treated with reverence.

The complete expression of the god-like qualities of the horse: a carving of
110 metres (374 feet), on a hillside at Uffington, Oxfordshire, possibly the tribal
symbol of the Atrebates, expressing here protection of the tribe and its lands.

Boar

The wild boar is ubiquitous in Celtic iconography and mythology. Dorsal bristles raised in blatant aggression, it appeared on coins, trumpets and helmet crests from England to Hungary and Romania. Its ferocity made it a natural warrior symbol, but its full significance was much greater: it was also the most common quarry of the Celtic hunter. As such, it enjoyed a special symbolic relationship with hunter gods; Ardwinna, the huntress deity of the Ardennes, is represented, dagger in hand, astride a wild boar. The boar was also associated with feasting and festivity, since its meat was particularly prized.

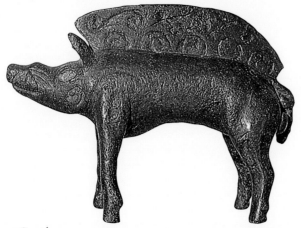

Bronze boar, Hungary, 2nd century BC.

Bull

aggression and strength were reckoned high virtues by the warrior Celts, and were qualities associated with their most potent animal symbols. The untamed bull was venerated in all the parts of Europe settled by the Celts, although its warlike connotations were tempered by the symbolism – that of agricultural plenty – associated with its domestic counterpart, the ox. The bull also seems to have been a symbol of fertility; there are records of the sacrifice of white bulls by Druids during fertility rites.

Bronze bull, Blansko, Czechoslovakia, 6th century BC.

Dog

dogs had three main areas of symbolic association for the Celts: hunting, healing and death. The healing connotation is especially intriguing: it was believed that cures for certain ailments could be effected by the application of canine saliva. The association with the hunt is an obvious one: dogs are depicted throughout Celtic Europe in the company of both hunters and huntresses, whom they aided in the pursuit of quarry and also protected. The Dutch goddess Nehalennia, a popular deity worshipped on the coast, is often shown with an especially friendly looking dog, who is playing the role of protector. The connection with death is clearly a reference to canine presences in the Otherworld; *The Mabinogion* relates that Arawn, a god of the underworld, was accompanied by a pack of white dogs with red ears.

Opposite Canine figures with rabbits depicted in the *Book of Kells*, AD *c.* 800.

arculis est dubit
se
aumgue uutas bona

ient apulsanua ap
IR uobis homo guensi

Horse

Symbol of speed, beauty and sexual prowess, the horse also had powerful religious connotations for the Celts: sacred images of horses abound in their art, from hill figures to stone carvings. The animal was closely associated with the Celtic sun god, who is often depicted on horseback on the stone columns of Gaul and western Germany. But the most famous Celtic horse deity was the fertility goddess Epona, patroness of cavalry officers. Iron Age coins also show images of horsewomen and female charioteers. As so many Celtic cults had associations with the horse it is probable that it was held in high reverence because of its innate qualities.

Left Horses were favourite subjects for Celtic coinage.

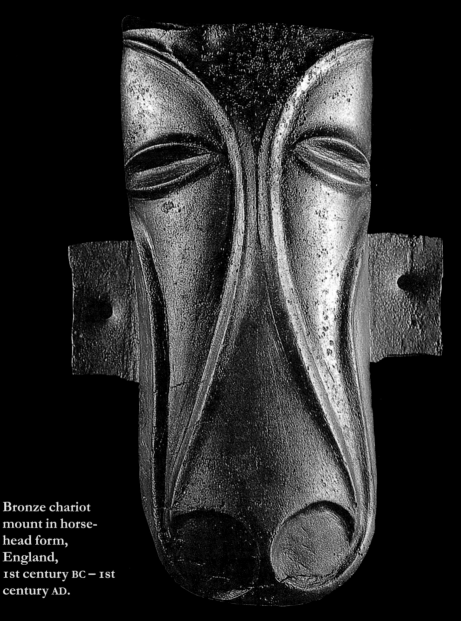

Bronze chariot
mount in horse-
head form,
England,
1st century BC – 1st
century AD.

Detail of a gold bracelet shaped like a ram, Germany, 5th century BC.

Ram

Yet another symbolic beast associated with the Celts' admiration of animal strength and aggression, the ram enjoyed cult status during the Romano-Celtic period. This was especially true in Gaul and Britain where it was associated with the Roman god Mercury, an association that derived directly from Classical mythology. But there is good reason to believe that the ram had a more purely warlike meaning for the Celts, since it was sometimes represented in the company of a war god.

A curious variant on ram symbolism was the ram-headed serpent, another example of the ambiguity and flexibility of Celtic thought. This strange hybrid, often shown in the company of the antlered god Cernunnos, combined the symbolism of fertility and aggression of the ram with the snake's association with both the underworld and renewal.

Stag

The Horned One, Cernunnos, 'Lord of all the Stags', was one of the most potent of all the Celtic zoomorphic gods. He is shown on one of the plates of the Gundestrup Cauldron *(opposite)*, seated in splendour, surrounded by symbols of fertility and plenty, accompanied by a stag and a ram-horned serpent. The symbolism of the stag went beyond obvious maleness and aggressive qualities; the spreading antlers associated the king of the forest with the trees because of the similarity in branching growth. And, like deciduous species of tree, the shedding of antlers in spring and autumn also made the stag the embodiment of the cyclical growth–decay–growth of nature. With the boar, the stag was the most prized quarry of hunters.

Eagle

another Celtic nature symbol that had strong Roman affiliations was the eagle, emblem of Jupiter, god of the skies. During the Romano-Celtic period the sun god of the Celts became merged with the Roman deity and took on the same associations, including that of the eagle. The magnificent wingspan of the bird and its ability to fly at great heights made it a natural companion for any deity of the heavens. In *The Mabinogion*, Lleu, a divine warrior, whose name means 'Bright One of the Skilful Hand', is struck a fatal blow, but immediately changes into an eagle and flies into an oak tree, the sacred tree of Jupiter.

Opposite Eagle and horse, two sacred beasts, on a Celtic coin.

THE SPIRIT

The objects that the Celts used in ceremony and even in everyday life were often rich in religious symbolism. Ornamental metalwork incorporated motifs of celestial significance: the wheel, swastika and spiral were attributes of a sky god, who controlled sun and lightning. The torc symbolized authority and often

OF THINGS

accompanied representations of gods. Cauldrons were especially prized and sometimes enjoyed the status of cult objects within a tribe; Irish myths tell of cauldrons of abundance, which seems to indicate their use in ritual feasting.

Gold arm-ring, Germany,
c. 4th century BC.

Boat

ritual and symbolism associated with boats was common among all the Celtic tribes of northwest Europe. Model boats in precious metals were made as offerings to the gods, especially those directly connected with the sea and water. A sea passage may also have suggested the journey of the soul to the Otherworld. Manannán Mac Lir, an Irish sea god with powers of magic and illusion, rode the waves like Poseidon in a horse-drawn chariot and carried Celtic heroes to the Otherworld beneath the sea.

Opposite A tiny gold boat of the 1st century BC, part of a larger hoard of precious objects, found at Broighter, County Derry, Northern Ireland.

The cauldron of rebirth

Ceremonial cooking vessels were central to the rituals of the Otherworld, the feasting associated with rebirth and resurrection. References to magic cauldrons abound in Celtic literature; one tale has it that the Irish possessed a cauldron into which their dead soldiers were thrown, then cooked at night to rise and fight again the next day. The Gundestrup Cauldron depicts a mythological narrative involving a wide range of gods and icons, including a bearded god served by two acolytes, and the solar wheel god with mythical beasts in attendance. It was found in a peat bog in Gundestrup, Denmark in 1891, and is made of partially gilded silver, with a large diameter of 69 centimetres (27 inches). The exact location and period of its manufacture remain unclear.

Above The Gundestrup Cauldron, Denmark, 1st–2nd century AD, made of decorated silver, may originally have been taken from Gaul to Denmark.

Opposite Detail of a bearded god flanked by smaller figures on the Gundestrup Cauldron.

Fire

For the chilly lands of northern Europe fire held a very special significance: it pushed back the outer darkness and brought warmth to tribal settlements. Ritual bonfires were lit to mark special occasions in the Celtic calendar such as Beltane, (1 May) and Samhain (1 November), the festivals celebrating the beginning and end of the growing season. Midsummer was also marked in both pagan and Christian periods by fire festivals. Several Classical commentators, including Julius Caesar, were struck by the use of fire in Celtic sacrificial rituals. As senior holy men, the Druids were responsible for public sacrifice to the gods; their victims were sometimes imprisoned in huge human-form wicker cages, which were then set alight.

Opposite A scene from the film, *The Wicker Man* (1973).

Bronze horned helmet,
England, 150–50 BC.
The helmet's large size
suggests it may have
been more ceremonial
than practical.

Helmet

For such a warlike people as the Celts, the weapons and accoutrements of the battlefield were obvious objects for veneration. Valuable military equipment was sometimes cast into water or marsh as a votive offering to the gods. It is likely, too, that some warriors were buried with their full regalia, and helmets of bronze and of iron with bronze decoration have been found in soldiers' graves. The helmet was itself a special object of significance and symbolism, presumably because of the high status accorded to the human head by the Celts. There are a number of examples in Celtic imagery of horned helmets, another way perhaps of representing deities in human form with horns.

The S-shape

The elaborate twists and intertwining of late Celtic art are only the most refined expression of a fascination with spirals, which goes back through the whole history of the Celts. In pagan times spiral and S-shaped symbols were associated with sky and solar cults. The solar god himself was sometimes represented carrying S-shaped objects, perhaps intended to represent lightning bolts.

Enamelled bronze dragonesque brooch, England, 1st century AD.

Swastika

One of the great enduring symbols of the whole of the ancient world, the swastika had wide currency as a sign of good luck and of solar beneficence. The motif occurs throughout the lands occupied by the Celts, sometimes on stonework in the company of images of the spoked wheel, another powerful sun symbol.

Torc

among the most magnificent figures depicted on the Gundestrup Cauldron is the 'Horned One', Cernunnos, with his branching antlers. Around his neck he wears a torc and he carries another. Other Celtic deities were depicted wearing or carrying torcs, almost certainly because this was a symbol of dignity and status. Important people were buried with torcs, and hoards of buried torcs and coins have been found, probably buried as offerings to a deity.

Opposite Gold torc, England, *c.* 75 BC. This is an object of complex fabrication, made of gold mixed with silver, with a diameter of 20 centimetres (8 inches).

Wheel

traditionally a religious icon in northern
Europe, by Romano-Celtic times the spoked
wheel had become a specific symbol of the
sun and the solar deities. Model wheels have
been found in graves, presumably buried with
the dead to help illuminate their journey to
the Otherworld. Certain cults also threw
miniature wheels into rivers and lakes as
offerings to the gods. The Celtic version
of Jupiter was especially associated with
the wheel; shrines devoted to his worship
sometimes also incorporate swastikas.

Opposite Detail of a wheel from the Gundestrup Cauldron.

THE CHRISTIAN

The massive movement of northern European people in the immediate post-Roman period effectively redrew the boundaries of the Celtic sphere of influence. Germanic people pushing westward across Europe eventually confined Celtic culture to the seaboard edges. During this period, too, Christianity spread among the Celtic tribes,

CELTS

especially in Ireland, inspiring a great flowering of the decorative arts. But the traditional motifs still recurred in manuscripts such as *The Book of Kells (below)*, inspired by the new religion. The ageless symbols of the Celts passed painlessly into the iconography of the new religion.

Cross

even in pre-Christian times the Celts had used the cross as a religious symbol. As in many other aspects of belief, the iconography and practice of the Christian church fitted easily with the pagan past – the cross could now take its place as a central motif in Celtic art. In Ireland, especially, the Christian era saw the height of stone cross making. The traditional Celtic skills of metalworking and jewelry were also put at the service of the new faith: this 12th-century oak and bronze cross *(opposite)* was made for Turlough O'Connor, High King of Ireland, to hold a relic of the True Cross.

Shrine

Although the Celts often chose natural places for religious activity – the sacred groves of druidical sacrifice – they also built structures, usually of great simplicity, for the same purpose. Such places were not venues for communal worship – any such activity would take place in the area outside – but rather sites for very specific ceremonies. For instance, the remains of offerings of weapon hoards and even animals have been found at shrine locations. This intense concentration of religious and symbolic experience in very specific places and objects continued unbroken among the western Celts into the Christian era.

Opposite Detail of the Shrine of the *Stowe Missal*, a bronze box which once housed an illuminated book, Ireland, 11th century.

A Celtic 'carpet'

The use of pagan motif and symbolism for the
Christian cause achieved one of its high points
in the so-called 'carpet' pages of the 7th-century
Book of Durrow (opposite). Traditional Celtic
interlace, trefoil designs and knots decorate
other pages of symbolic representations of the
four Evangelists, although the imagery of both
men and animals is non-naturalistic, very much
in the mode of earlier, non-Christian art. There
is also a striking resemblance on the 'carpet'
pages to the patterns of earlier Celtic metalwork.

The Book of Kells

Probably the greatest artistic achievement of the Celtic world, *The Book of Kells* (*c.* 800) is a mine of complex symbolism. There are the Christian symbols for the four Evangelists: the man for Matthew, the lion for Mark, the calf for Luke and the eagle for John, which are represented throughout the manuscript. But intertwined with this imagery are distinctively Celtic motifs; the rosette, symbol of the sun, spirals, knots and interlacing. Animal symbolism, too, is introduced at every possible opportunity: fish, cats, mice, hens, snakes, dragons and birds.

Above Detail of men from *The Book of Kells*.

Opposite Detail from *The Book of Kells* of the Chi Ro monogram, the first two letters in the Greek spelling of 'Christ'.

Native Americans

FIRST ENCOUNTERS

BERING STRAIT

Point Hope

South Alaskan
Eskimo

Koyukon

Tanana

Ingalik Tanaina

Chugach

Ahtena

Aleut

Tlingit

Haida Queen
Charlotte Island

Kwakiuti

Nootka

Makah

Chinook

Tillamoc

Coos Karok
Yurok Hupa

Yuki Pomo

Miwok

Costano

Chumash

Gabrielir

5

W hen the first European explorers came
to the North American continent in the
early 16th century, they were setting foot on
a colossal landmass with an indigenous and
varied population of over a million
inhabitants. Between the Atlantic and
Pacific existed a diversity and richness
of culture, which expressed itself vividly
in legend, ritual
and symbolism.

Left The symbolic
power of birds of
prey: the feather
headdress of a
Plains chief.

**The Peoples of
North America**

1a Arctic
1b Subarctic
2 Great Plains
3 Northeast
4 Southeast
5 California
6 Great Basin
7 Southwest
8 Northwest Coast
9 Plateau

RITUAL AND SYMBOL

Traditional Native American mythology and religion are inextricably intertwined; their visible elements are ritual and symbol. From the external evidence we see the major concerns: the creation of the earth and its people, the search for the favours of nature through contact with spirits, and the acquisition of personal dignity and power. To benefit the tribe, objects – such as the medicine pipe of the Blackfoot – animals and places were vested with symbolic meaning.

The Californian Maidu vision of the beginnings of the universe is one of primeval waters on which floats a raft with Turtle and Father of the Secret Society. They are joined by Earth Initiate, who is invited by Turtle to make the dry land of the earth.

Opposite The Blackfoot medicine pipe was brought out from its bundle on the sound of the first thunder in spring as a talismanic protection for the tribe.

The Skeena River, Northwest Coast, where the Kitksan believed
that encounters with supernatural spirits took place.

**The Maidu version of the creation of humankind has Earth
Initiate, in cooperation with Coyote, first fashioning all the other
animals and then making two figures – one man, one woman.**

THE HOLY LAND

The symbolism of Native Americans is characterized by reverence for the environment. Everything in the natural world has its own spirit, its own life. Clothes and artefacts are symbolically significant because they take on the qualities of the animals and materials from which they are made. And the land itself is alive with spirit and symbol: mountains and valleys, deserts and rivers all have their sacred sites, where the energies of the universe can be contacted and the health and prosperity of the tribe ensured.

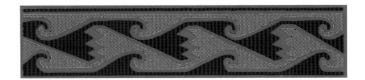

THE BIRTH OF THE PEOPLES

Two symbolic beasts recur constantly in the varied creation accounts of Native Americans: the coyote and the turtle. The former is often coupled with the figure of the Old Man as prime mover in the whole process of bringing the earth into being. Another theme that recurs is that of an animal diving into the primordial waters to bring up mud to make the earth.

The turtle as a shield (*opposite*) and pouch (*left*), Cheyenne, Great Plains.

O-kee-pa

Opposite The Bull Dance, part of the O-kee-pa ceremony in a Mandan village of the Great Plains, as recorded by the artist-explorer George Catlin in 1832.

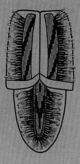

myth and legend were the means by which the tribes explained their own history and that of the world at large. Among the tribes of the Great Plains, for instance, various ceremonies, including the famous Sun Dance, alluded to the generation and regeneration of the world. The most extraordinary ritual, however, was the O-kee-pa ceremony of the Mandans, which told of the creation of the world and its inhabitants and the forging of the character of the Mandan tribe. The fight to establish the tribe was symbolized by suspending young volunteer participants some feet from the ground by means of splints passed through the chest or back.

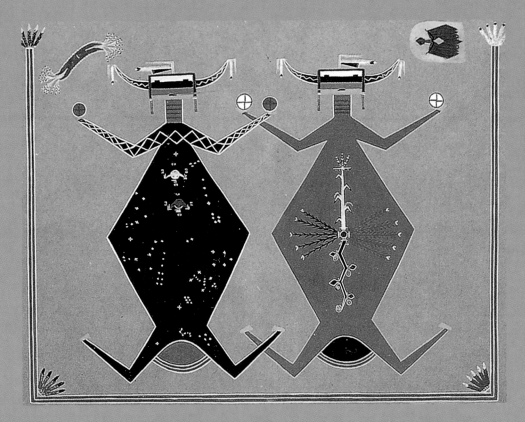

Above Father Sky (black) and Mother Earth (blue) in a Navajo sand painting made to celebrate the healing ceremony of Shootingway.

Mother Earth and Father Sky

many Native American myths and legends refer to a primary deity: the Creator of the people of the Northwest Coast, the Father Sun of the Plateau Nez Perce, and the Old Man or First Worker of the Plains Crow. Often there is interaction between the heavens and the earth, the male principle being associated with the sun and the female with the earth and its produce. The Apache god Usen, for instance, has the power to repopulate the world after disaster. In Navajo painting and weaving Father Sky is associated with the sun and other heavenly bodies, while Mother Earth is shown with the produce of the earth.

For the Zuni, the original creator, Awonawilona, first took on the form of the sun, then made the clouds, whence came the sea, which interacted with his light to create Mother Earth.

Sun Dance

The self-torture of the Mandan O-kee-pa ceremony recurred in various forms in the Sun Dances of other Plains tribes. Young men would be harpooned by skewers through skin and muscle and hoisted above the ground – an act of bravery and suffering in recognition of the sun's beneficence. Traditionally performed in June when the sun was highest and the day longest, the dance was a means of thanking the sun for its protection in the past and requesting that this should continue long into the future.

The Cherokee saw the sun as female and living on the other side of the arch of the heavens. Her daughter, however, lived in the sky directly above the earth, where she would be visited every day by her mother who would pause in her cycle for dinner with her offspring.

Opposite Hide painting of the Sun Dance ceremony, probably Sioux, Great Plains.

Duality

among the Apache and Navajo of the Southwest there was a myth that the Earth Mother bore twin sons who were instrumental in continuing the creation of land and people. The involvement of two brothers recurs constantly in creation myths, recalling the Hero Twins of Maya legend, sometimes as the primary force at the inception of the world. The Diegueño people of southern California believed that the two brothers emerged from the primordial salt sea, then created land, followed by the moon and the sun, and finally by man and woman.

Right A concern with dual forces sprang from environments and lives of dramatic contrasts: an early Mogollon pottery bowl with two symbolic figures, possibly the male and female principles or life and death.

The Menominee of the Northeast believed that Manabozho, a hero, was given a twin brother in the form of a wolf, who was later drowned when the ice on a lake gave way under him. The sounds of Manabozho's grief caused ripples which formed the hills on the earth's surface.

The stars above

Sky powers are especially prominent in North American myth, and none more so than the Morning Star and the Evening Star. The Pawnee in particular brought cosmology to Great Plains culture, using buckskin charts of the heavens in divination and the foretelling of the future. Until the early 19th century the Pawnee practised human sacrifice to symbolize the overcoming of the Evening Star by the Morning Star. A young girl from the tribe – a personification of the Evening Star – would be killed by an arrow through the heart, leaving the heavens to the rule of the Morning Star.

Opposite A 19th-century costume for the Ghost Dance, a ceremony intended to preserve Native American culture, Arapaho, Great Plains.

Thunderbird

The Plateau Chilcotin saw Thunder as a powerful celestial chief; he had three daughters who were desired by all earthly young men. But whenever one asked for the hand of a daughter he would be tricked by Thunder into entering a bear's den and killed.

great symbolic importance was everywhere ascribed to the voice of Thunder, sometimes considered only second to the original creative impulse in power and influence. It was usually seen figuratively as a large bird, although the legends of the Northern Paiute refer to a Thunder Badger, with the power to cause thunder, lightning and rain. The great supernatural power wielded by the Thunderbird was sometimes represented by two great horns, which sprang from the upper part of its head. Its lair would usually be some mountain fastness in the territory of a particular tribe.

Tree and totem

At the centre of a Plains village there was an open space reserved for ceremonial and ritual dance. Its centrepiece might be a sacred cedar post, a totem symbolizing the First Man and the ancestors of the tribe. Trees or poles were seen to inspire great spiritual strength by many peoples; the founding of the league of five nations of the Iroquois was symbolized by the carving of a great Tree of Peace, a totem placed in the territory of the Onondaga as a focal point for meetings. Sometimes the Northeast tribes represented the Tree of Peace as springing directly from the back of the Creator Turtle and linking all levels of the universe as an *axis mundi*.

Opposite Ceremonial totem poles, Northwest Coast. The detail *(below)*, representing the 'Man of the Wilds', the spirit name of a chief, is taken from an especially tall example, Tsimshian, Northwest Coast.

SPRITUAL POWERS

There was an awareness among the Native American peoples that the world around them could be malevolent and violent. To ensure survival and, indeed, prosperity in such an environment, the individual would attempt to placate the many spirits inhabiting his universe. These were seen to take on both the insubstantial forms of nature and location spirits and the more solid incarnation of favoured animals, each symbolizing a range of qualities, a symbolism which the individual could extend to himself by incorporating the most potent parts of any creature into his own apparel.

Opposite A war cap of buffalo horn and feathers from predatory birds brought the spiritual powers of those creatures to the wearer, Blackfoot, Great Plains.

Spirits of nature

every aspect of the external world, animate and inanimate, is imbued with spirit essences. The mythologies of the Southwest tribes, notably the Zuni and Hopi, are peopled with spirits of natural phenomena who help to regulate fertility and rainfall and maintain order in the running of the universe. Their presence is celebrated by dances which are both a thanksgiving and a plea for health and plenty in the future. All peoples celebrated spiritual forces at work in nature; some could be malevolent, causing storms and disaster, while more benevolent ones would be enlisted by shamans to bolster their magical powers.

Opposite A Zuni *kachina* doll, Southwest. For the Zuni and Hopi the *kachinas* were spirits who would stay with the tribe for over half the year before returning to their mountain homes; they brought well-being and rain, and were therefore celebrated in frequent dances and ceremonies.

Immortals and little people

The peoples of the Southeast, notably the Cherokee and Choctaw, were forced to make a harrowing resettlement from their lands to Oklahoma in the late 1830s. Solace for their terrible experience, which they referred to as the 'Trail of Tears', would have been provided by their rich culture: legends telling of tribe members being rescued in the wilderness by benevolent sprites, the Little People, who would provide them with food and clothing. Another category of protectors were the *nunnehi*, the immortals who dwelt in lakes and rocks, and who later vainly attempted to put the tribe beyond the reach of the white man.

Opposite This wooden mask was worn by the Cherokee in the Booger dance to frighten off enemy tribes, and later Europeans.

Eagle and hawk

The single, dominant carving of an eagle atop a soaring mortuary pole of the Northwest Haida is potent testimony to the symbolic power of great birds in Native American culture. Further south, the Hopi believed in a kind of eagle heaven, where the birds went to breed before returning to earth. The Plains Sioux attached eagle and hawk feathers to their accoutrements of war and headdresses to partake of the ferocious attacking powers of the birds. Eagle and hawk were also associated by many tribes with the all-powerful Thunderbird; feather capes worn by the Cherokee were intended to confer the attributes of the bird on the wearer.

Testimonies to the war like qualities of the eagle: an eagle crest headdress *(above)* with abalone inlaid eye, Tsimshian, Northwest Coast. Each feather on the war bonnet *(opposite)* of Chief Yellow Calf, the last chief of the Great Plains Arapaho, signified a war honour.

Bear

The animals of North America were all invested with a symbolic dimension by the tribes. Yet, despite much distancing from daily life, many of them – especially the bear – were seen to be very close to man, offering help and sustenance. Certain Californian tribes, for instance, regarded the bear as being so close to them that they would not eat its flesh, but would use the skin to make clothing, which would confer the characteristics of the bear on the wearer. On the Northwest Coast prayers were offered to the bear before a hunt and, after a bear had been killed, the head and skin would be formally laid out.

Opposite The entrance to a tribal house on Chief Shakes Island is represented by the womb of a mother bear totem, Tlingit, Northwest Coast.

Many peoples of North America told legends of humans mating with animals: buffalo-wives, bear-women, deer-women, eagle- and whale-husbands. The Blackfoot have a tale of a young woman who is discovered to have a bear as a lover; he is killed by the girl's family, who are then all killed by the vengeful daughter.

Wolf

a ruthless hunter, the wolf also had a mythological dimension for the tribes of the Plains. For the Blackfoot it was intimately associated with tales of the creation and the original Old Man who used a wolf to produce the configurations of the earth's surface: at each place that the animal stopped on the mud a valley appeared, while the remainder of the surface became the mountains and plains. On the Northwest Coast the winter ritual of *klukwana*, an induction ceremony, was supposedly conducted by supernatural wolves.

Opposite A very early (800–1400) wolf head effigy, Southeast.

Serpents and snakes

One of the most extraordinary sites in the whole of North America is the Serpent Mound on an Ohio hilltop; a half-kilometre earthwork in the form of a serpent clasping a hemispherical mound in its jaws. The monumentality of the work indicates the central position occupied by the Great Serpent in the symbolism of Native Americans. Among the Cherokee and other tribes of the Southeast he was known as Uktena, malevolent but also the bearer of a crystal, which, when used by a shaman, brought prosperity to those lands after his death.

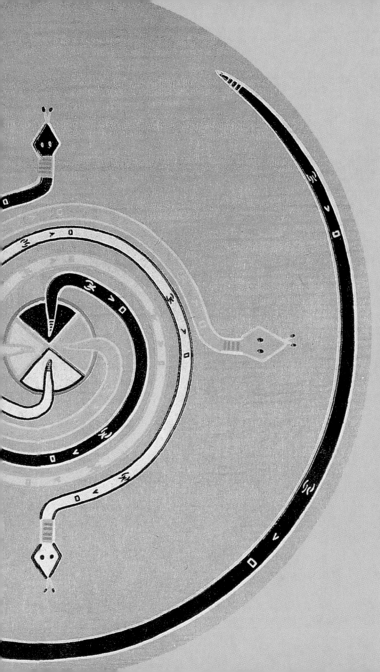

Left Snakes, especially the rattler, are very much revered among the peoples of the Southwest: a Navajo sand painting.

Above A Hopi shaman gathers up snakes in preparation for the famous Snake Dance to bring summer rain.

Buffalo

Of the many hardships inflicted on the Plains Indians by the westward expansion of white settlers there were few greater than the massive destruction of the great buffalo herds. For the peoples of the Plains the buffalo was a potent symbol of beneficence; after all, it had provided them with meat, clothing and shelter since time immemorial through its flesh and hide. Even during the pre-horse period, there were annual and semi-annual hunts in which all members of the tribe – men, women and children – would take part in driving a whole herd into a compound or over a cliff.

Opposite A rattle decorated with the image of a buffalo; such rattles were used to emulate the sounds of the animal with which the participants in a ritual wished to be brought into contact, Great Plains.

In Comanche legend Coyote was credited with the presence of buffalo on earth. All the buffalo originally belonged to an old woman and her young cousin, but Coyote succeeded in infiltrating their pen with a small animal whose howling so alarmed the buffalo that they broke out to roam the earth.

Raven

Yet another creature invested in legend with powers associated with the creation, the raven – the Trickster – was very much an icon of the peoples of the Northwest Coast. As a culture hero, he occupied the position of secondary creator, bringing the sun, moon, stars and other substantial forces into being. The epithet of Trickster, however, refers to his role as a joker, with a predilection for stealing food and sex – appetites that often resulted in his own humiliation. After attempting one subterfuge on an immortal man known as Petrel, the latter was so incensed that he chased the Trickster up a tree and then lit a fire beneath it, thus turning the raven's feathers black, and so they have remained ever since.

Opposite A chest in argillite carved by Charles Edenshaw, the most famous of the late 19th-century Haida carvers. The figure of the raven on the lid has both human and bird features, Northwest Coast.

Antlered beasts

among the animals considered especially spiritual and having great symbolic significance were the great antlered mammals: deer, caribou and elk. In northwest California, the White Deerskin Dance, which might engage its participants for as long as two weeks, celebrated the renewal of the world. Among the warriors of the Plains the male elk symbolized much that was desirable in a young man – beauty, great strength and, seemingly, an ability to attract females to him at will – hence the animal's association with courtship ritual among the Sioux. Further north, among the Inuit of the Arctic, the caribou was especially revered as the principal source of meat.

Opposite A serving dish carved with the figures of three caribou, Inuit, Arctic.

Horse

the horse was a relative latecomer to Plains culture. It became, however, one of the great iconic beasts of the most powerful tribes of the central part of the continent, often turning village-based farmers into buffalo-hunting nomads and leading ultimately to the formation of the warrior groups which had their finest martial hour on the Little Bighorn in 1876. Originally introduced through Spanish missions in the Southwest, the horse was first used by the peoples of the Great Basin and the Plateau, becoming highly integrated into the religious symbolism of, notably, the Nez Perce.

The Nez Perce were among the first Native Americans to acquire the horse, developing a breed known as the 'Appaloosa', which still exists today.

Opposite A hide painting depicting a horse-stealing raid, Great Plains.

Aquatic creatures

Water and its denizens feature in many creation myths. In the Southeast, Water Beetle dredged up the primeval mud to create the earth, while Water Spider brought fire. Among the Dakota, though an inland people, monsters of the deep were especially feared and thought to be the enemies of Thunderbird. But it was among the coastal peoples of the Northwest that, understandably, the most elaborate and complex symbolism involving marine life existed. The killer whale was worshipped by the Tlingit and Haida who believed the drowned became whales themselves.

Opposite A shaman's rattle carved in the form of a head of a killer whale, Haida, Northwest Coast.

The Subarctic Tahltan tell the story of a fisherman's wife who accidentally kills a killer whale. The other whales then pull her under the water and take her to be their slave. Only with the help of a shark is the fisherman able to rescue his wife.

THE GOOD EARTH

Gratitude for the bounty of the earth runs as a constant vein through Native American mythology, legend and symbolism. Animals, plant life and the earth itself are possessed of spirits and interact with the humans of their territory. This vision of the whole environment as symbolically charged probably reached its most intense form among the Plains Indians, perhaps because of the extraordinary physical power of their lands – hills, valleys and great rivers, all teeming with wildlife, as well as the great sky above, itself a symbol of the power of the universe.

Opposite The natural bounty of the Great Plains, Indian territory in Wyoming.

Holy mountain

The mythologizing of the environment was carried to the point of regarding the whole land as a living being and all exceptional features, such as mountains, as concentrations of spiritual power. For the Blackfoot in Montana, Chief Mountain owed its location to the Old Man, the first creative force, who had created it to demonstrate his power to the Great Spirit. Mount Hood, a dormant volcano in Oregon, was thought by the Cayuse to have been the place of origin of fire.

Opposite Chief Mountain in northern Montana was a sacred place to the Blackfoot, who would visit to commune with spirits.

Emergence

The place of emergence of a tribe is central to its
mythology, the explanation of its very existence, and
it may very well be identified as a specific location.
For the Hopi of the Southwest desert it is the floor
of the Grand Canyon, to which their ancestors
would return after death and where they could
communicate with their creator. The Navajo have
a similar emergence myth, celebration of which
forms part of the Blessingway ceremony.

Opposite A Blessingway sand painting celebrating the emergence
of the Navajo nation, Southwest.

Overleaf A very sacred place: the Grand Canyon, birthplace of the Hopi.

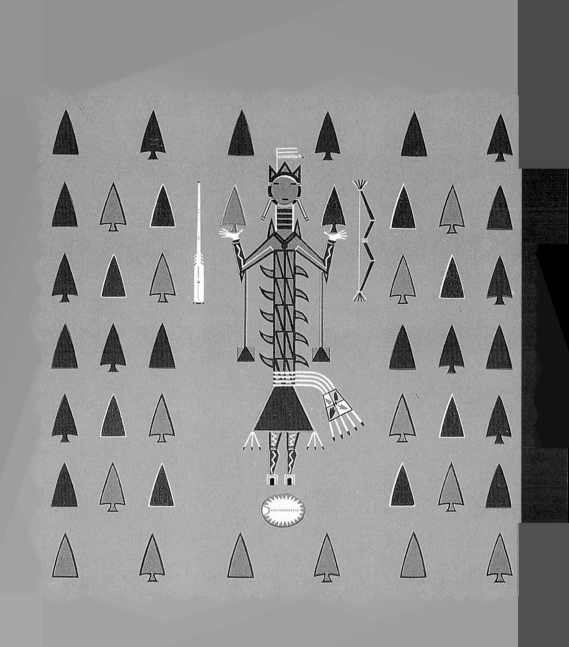

Vision quest

among the peoples of the Plains
especially, the sacred high places of
their territories played a significant
part in the initiation rites of young
men. After purification rituals in the
village or encampment the young
initiate would set out to a remote
place, such as a mountain top, there
to experience the rigours of the
environment, to fast and to commune
with the spirits. This quest for
visionary help could be repeated
later in life, especially if the individual
was seeking to enhance shamanistic
powers. Within the community too,
special lodges in which spiritual
purification could take place were
set up, using the materials of the
natural world.

Opposite The
framework of a
sweat lodge on Bear
Butte, South Dakota,
where initiates would
sit around fire pits in
which stones were
heated. Water would
then be sprinkled
on the stones to
produce vapour
to aid communion
with the spirits.

Falling water

just as mountains and high places held concentrations of spiritual power, so other major physical phenomena were incorporated into the legends of many tribes. Such a monumental feature as Niagara Falls, for instance, symbolized nothing less than the victory of good over evil for the Iroquoian peoples of the Northeast. The falls were created after the defeat by Thunder of a monster water snake, which had persistently brought sickness to a Seneca village. After its death from the lightning bolts hurled by Thunder, its body became lodged in rocks in the Niagara River, forcing the waters to pour over it in a triumphant cascade.

Opposite Good triumphs over evil: the symbolic victory of the Niagara Falls.

The sea, the sea

the munificence of the land reflected in the legends of the peoples of the Plains finds a parallel in the sea myths and symbolism of the coastal tribes. Even non-coastal communities have many stories of underwater monsters, but it is in the lands along the Northwest Coast that the most vivid tales are told – hardly surprising since the sea has

always been the main food source. Among the Tlingit, Tsimshian and Haida, the main monster is a bringer of prosperity, with claws and teeth of copper, the local symbol of wealth. The sea itself it associated with bounty, which comes from the Great Chief Under the Water, an all-controlling supernatural being known as the Copper Maker.

Opposite According to legend, the raven created these islands from the spray he caused to rise from the primeval waters, Haida, Queen Charlotte Islands, Northwest Coast. The Haida shamans often used rattles carved in the form of a sea monster *(above).*

SHAMAN AND CEREMONY

The most famous shaman or 'medicine man' was Sitting Bull of the Teton Dakota. As a war leader he was regarded as having almost god-like powers, especially after he joined with Crazy Horse to defeat General Custer at the battle of the Little Bighorn in 1876. It was his assassination in 1890 that led directly to the last battle of the Plains, the massacre at Wounded Knee in South Dakota. The art of the shaman was to acquire power within a tribe by forming special relationships with groups of spirits, often animals.

The equipment of shamans may very well include an amulet *(above)*, representing the creatures they wish to draw on for power – here a bird with a humanoid figure – and a collection of staff, rattle, necklace and bear claw crown *(opposite)*, Tsimshian, Northwest Coast.

Medicine man

Opposite An Eskimo carving shows a shaman with two animal helpers; a drum, used to summon spirits, is beside him.

Below A figurine of the spirit of a shaman, leaving his body to fly to other parts of the world, Eskimo, Arctic.

Overleaf An elegantly carved shamanistic pipe, Eskimo, Arctic *(left)*. A shaman's storage chest carved with the face of the moon, Tsimshian, Northwest Coast *(right)*.

Within a Native American community – from the deepest south to the very north of the continent – the principal role of the shaman was to look to the health of the tribe on both general and particular levels. On the general level he had to interpret the symbolism and meaning of the world around – to encourage crops, predict the weather and act as fortune-teller. He was also the local doctor; among the Navajo, for instance, most shamanistic ceremonies were devoted to the relief of individual illnesses and pain.

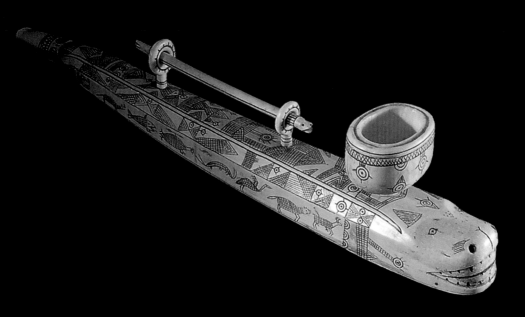

Soul catcher

the shaman would make use of many aids (possibly carried in a chest) to achieve his goal of health for the individual and the tribal unit. Communal pipe smoking, notably among the Plains Lakota, symbolized a search for peace and the sealing of agreements. In curing the sick his most important aid was the soul catcher to restore the soul to the body of the sick person; it was widely believed that illness was caused by the escape of the soul from the patient, who could only be cured by its return.

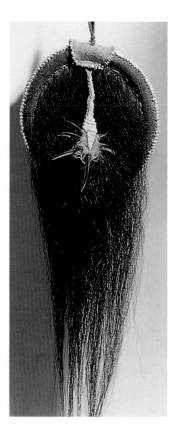

Opposite A soul catcher made of bone and abalone, Tlingit, Northwest Coast.

Right An especially potent talisman: a scalp stretched on a wooden hoop, Great Plains.

A special place

Opposite Places of normal habitation during much of the year, the long houses of the Haida, Northwest Coast, were used for sacred ceremonials in winter (reconstruction).

even among the nomadic peoples of North America, special shelters and lodges, perhaps attended by elaborate totems, were built for celebratory feasts, dances and shamanistic ritual. Around the Great Lakes are various sacred sites associated with the Grand Medicine Society, which, as its name implies, was concerned with the curative function of the shaman. But perhaps the most extraordinary evidence of such ceremonial lodges is the circle of boulders on Medicine Mountain in Wyoming, a 'medicine wheel' which is probably the remains of a Sun Dance lodge.

Medicine bundle

The acquisition of power and strength from the denizens of the animal world was not simply a matter of communicating with their souls; their unique qualities could also be passed on through their skins, feathers or even whole bodies. The skin or carcass of an animal or bird would then be wrapped in cloth and the whole bundle suspended by straps during the ritual. The Crow placed great value on eagle bundles, while the Blackfoot revered the beaver.

Above A weasel medicine bundle, Crow, Great Plains.

Opposite Masks such as this were used during Grand Medicine Society rituals to appease spirits, Iroquois, Northeast.

Sand painting

another exciting form of spirit attraction is sand
painting, unique in North America to the nations
of the Southwest, especially the Navajo, who
have survived perhaps more successfully as an
entity than any other Native American people.
Their craft traditions, still vigorous to this day,
are expressed in fine weaving and in their quite
remarkable sand paintings. These are traditionally
made on the floor of the residence *(hogan)*,
using sand and charcoal as the main materials.
The subjects depicted are the spirits whose
powers are to be invoked.

Opposite An early 20th-century sand painting symbolizing
the creation, Navajo, Southwest.

The ultimate ritual

dance could be regarded as the ultimate expression of symbolism among Native American peoples: it celebrates the beneficence of nature in animal dances; it ensures the cohesion of the community in its re-enactment of the deeds of ancestors and therefore the birth of peoples; it assures the success of the hunt for the

nomad and a flourishing harvest for the farmer. Remnants of pottery of the prehistoric Hohokam civilization which flourished in the deserts of Arizona, show ceremonial dancers wearing symbolic headdresses – the human being impersonating and imploring the forces of nature, the source of North American legend.

Dance, the ultimate symbol of the well-being of a community, noted by John White in this drawing made in Virginia in the 1580s *(above)* and this early potsherd (500–900) *(opposite)*, Hohokam, Arizona, Southwest.

The Maya

THE MAYA

The Spanish Conquest was foreseen by the Maya prophet Chilam Balam: 'Receive your guests, the bearded men, the men of the East, the bearers of the sign of God, lord.'

Opposite Map of the lands occupied by the Maya, showing the principal sites.

Page 246 Mayan courtly ritual: musicians portrayed in a mural at Bonampak, AD 790.

Modern commentaries term the area in which the ancient Maya lived as Mesoamerica, characterized both as a geographical region and as a cultural entity. Its peoples shared the 260-day calendar, various elements of religious practice and belief – including blood-letting and human sacrifice – and a sense of common culture, manifested in agriculture, architecture and even game playing. The principal lands of the Maya – a society driven by ritual and symbolism – lay in the Yucatán Peninsula, in present-day Mexico, Guatemala, Belize and Honduras.

Isla Cerritos

Komchen

Dzibilchaltun   Izamal

Mayapan   Chichen Itza

Oxkintok   Coba

Uxmal   Kabah   Tulum

Sayil   Labna   Island of Cozumel

NORTHERN LOWLANDS

QUINTANA ROO

Edzna

GULF OF MEXICO

CAMPECHE

Xicalango

Candelaria River

Becan

Usumacinta River

Rio Bec   Hondo River

Calakmul   Nohmul Cuello   Cerros

TABASCO

El Mirador   Rio Azul   Lamanai

CARIBBEAN SEA

Palenque

Nakbe   San Jose

Uaxactun   Holmul   Belize River

Tikal

CHIAPAS

Piedras Negras   Barton Ramie

Yaxchilan   SOUTHERN LOWLANDS

Bonampak   Pasión River

Altar de Sacricios   Seibal

Dos Pilas

NORTHERN HIGHLANDS   Lake Izabal

Naco

Quirigua

Izapa   Copan

PACIFIC OCEAN   SOUTHERN HIGHLANDS

Kaminaljuyu

Mexico
Guatemala
Belize
El Salvador
Honduras

Cities and sites

Unlike other cultures in Mesoamerica, the Maya flourished in a multiplicity of centres. One substantial reason for this was the ability of the various communities to communicate through an ever more sophisticated language of great symbolic richness. By the Classic period competing city-states had emerged all over the Maya lands: Bonampak, Caracol, Copán, Piedras Negras, Tikal and, eventually, the great centre of Palenque. In the 9th century AD, however, the wealth and power of the Maya seem to have suffered rapid collapse, leaving only separate regional centres to flourish until the Spanish Conquest. By this time the Maya cities often had several layers of buildings and remains.

Tikal, Guatemala, from the air.

The city of Tikal covered 15.5 square kilometres (6 square miles) and comprised about 3,000 structures, ranging from temples to huts; estimates of the total population vary between 10,000 and 40,000.

Time and the Maya

The history of the Maya is divided into three periods: the Preclassic, from 1500 BC until AD 200; the Classic, AD 200–900; and the Postclassic, from AD 900 to the Spanish Conquest in the 16th century. The Maya reckoned time by two calendars: Long Count or Calendar Round. Long Count dates were derived from a 360-day year, known as a *tun*, divided into 18 months of 20 days. The Calendar Round had two versions: the *haab* of 365 days, and the *tzolkin* of 260 days.

A schematic representation of the Maya Calendar Round.

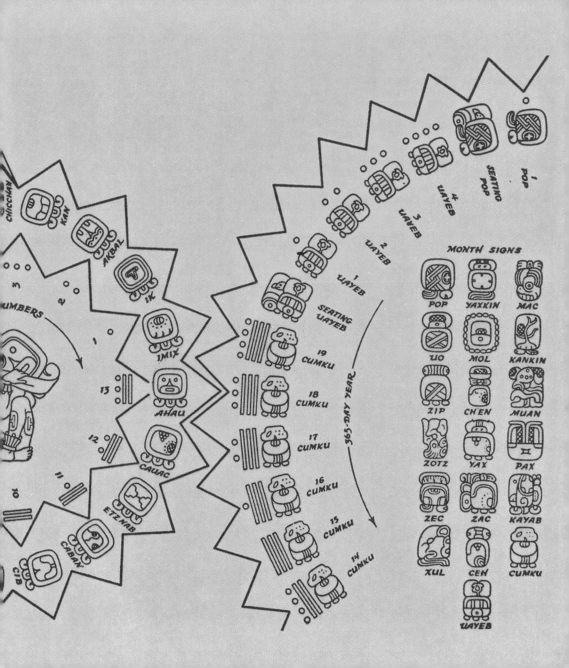

CHICCHAN

KAN

AKBAL

IK

NUMBERS

IMIX

AHAU

CAUAC

ETZ NAB

CABAN

CIB

SEATING UAYEB

1 UAYEB

2 UAYEB

3 UAYEB

4 UAYEB

SEATING POP

1 POP

19 CUMKU

18 CUMKU

17 CUMKU

16 CUMKU

15 CUMKU

14 CUMKU

365-DAY YEAR

MONTH SIGNS

POP

YAXKIN

MAC

UO

MOL

KANKIN

ZIP

CHEN

MUAN

ZOTZ

YAX

PAX

ZEC

ZAC

KAYAB

XUL

CEH

CUMKU

UAYEB

A language of symbols

Symbol and metaphor pervaded the whole of the Maya way of life and the methods of recording it. All levels of the universe, from natural objects and animals to the super-natural, carried a great weight of association and significance. The carvings on stelae, one of our primary sources of information about the Maya, reveal a world of multi-layered meaning. A house, a maize field, a great caiman or even a tortoise could represent the earth. The hieroglyphic writing of the Maya, itself a complex series of symbols, refers consistently to a world of ritual: blood-letting, accession, birth, burial and kingship.

Approximately 85 per cent of Classic Maya inscriptions can now be read, making the civilization the only historical one in the New World with comprehensive records, stretching back to the 3rd century AD.

Opposite A leaf from the *Dresden Codex* – the most extensive surviving pre-Columbian codex – reproduced in Alexander von Humboldt's atlas of the New World, Paris, 1810.

THE SACRED COSMOS

To the Maya the universe was wholly alive with spiritual power and symbolism: all natural phenomena, supernatural beings and humans played connecting parts in one great cosmic ritual. The overall context for this action was viewed as a three-part structure: the Overworld, the Middleworld and the Underworld. The first was probably viewed as the day sky, illuminated by the sun, but the night sky was identified with the Underworld which therefore was seen to pass over humanity daily. This was of particular significance to the Maya who regarded the movement of heavenly bodies as indicative of the actions of the gods. The Middleworld was that of humans, with the four cardinal points of the compass each designated by a specific tree, bird and colour.

cosmos, a complex structure of symbolism and ritual,

The sacred tree

The three levels of the Maya universe were joined by a central tree, an *axis mundi*, its roots plunging into the Underworld and its branches reaching to the Overworld, the heavens. This central tree was associated with the colour green, while four additional trees of the Middleworld, signifying the cardinal directions, were designated by red, white, black and yellow. The red tree signified the east and the rising sun; the white, the north and the ancestral dead; the yellow, the south, right hand of the sun; the black, the west, the setting sun and the Underworld.

Opposite The Tree of Life is shown growing from the king's body on the sarcophagus lid of Pakal's tomb (d. 31 August 683), Temple of Inscriptions, Palenque, Mexico.

By the late Classic period Maya sculptors had begun to excel at low relief carving, displaying a new dynamism in figure work.

Creation

befitting a people obsessed with calendars and time, the Maya were very precise in their placing of the creation of the world, the final version of which was thought to have begun on 13 August 3114 BC. They also believed that the world had been created and destroyed at least three times. The most important surviving sacred book of the Maya, the *Popol Vuh*, recounts that creation took place through dialogue between the gods Tepeu and Gukumatz, whereby the earth was raised up from the primordial sea. After failed attempts at sculpting humans out of mud and wood, the gods successfully created mankind out of maize, which became a sacred crop for the Maya.

A symbol of creation, the maize god Hun Hunahpu rises from a turtle's back, a symbol of the earth, encircled by the Hero Twins, on a plate dating from the 8th century AD.

The Hero Twins

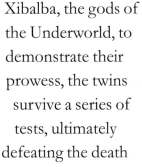

a number of deities and mythological figures appear as pairs or triads in Maya art and legend. The most famous of these were the Hero Twins, Hunahpu and Xbalanque, whose adventures are recounted in the *Popol Vuh*, the most thorough account of the creation of the Maya people and the birth of their religion. The twins were notably expert in the Maya ballgame; summoned by the lords of Xibalba, the gods of the Underworld, to demonstrate their prowess, the twins survive a series of tests, ultimately defeating the death gods. The last stage of this contest sees the twins perform a series of apparent miracles, bringing the dead back to life. The lords of the Underworld beg to be sacrificed so that they too can experience the return to life. The twins comply, but omit the resurrection!

Opposite The meeting of the Hero Twins with the god Itzamna depicted on a yellow and orange painted vase, Mexico, *c.* 593–830.

The earth

One common metaphor for the
earth in the Maya bestiary was
the caiman, evoking the image of
mountainous land floating on the
original waters of creation.
The varied phenomena of
the earth – mountains,
rivers, earth itself,
caves and sky – were all
thought by the Maya to
have their own intense
spiritual life. Another model
for the earth was the maize
field, the growing of which
symbolized the creation
of the Maya
world and
people.

A tripod pot with lid; the handle is in the form of a spotted turtle,
a common symbol of the earth, Guatemala, *c*. 495–593.

Above This section of a late Classic cylinder vase shows the Three Stone Place (a deity is sitting on three stones) where the gods created the universe by separating the heavens from earth, *c.* 672–830.

Opposite Skybands included symbols for the various heavenly bodies, and represented the belief that the sky was divided into numerous distinct zones.

The heavens

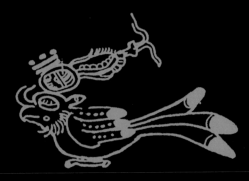

The skies were a deep source of mystery to the Maya, a realm of supernatural happenings with which they associated some of their most potent symbolism. The harpy eagle and the muan bird, a horned owl, were both symbols of the sky and of the twenty-year *katun* period. In common with other Mesoamerican civilizations, the Maya believed the sky to be supported by the Skybearers, four gods – all brothers – who each upheld one of the four corners of the sky.

Throughout the year the Maya conducted rites and ceremonies to urge the heavens to provide the conditions to increase the abundance of crops and game.

Sun

The Maya had a special regard for the sun and associated some of their most powerful gods and animal deities with it: both the jaguar and the eagle were solar creatures. A sign for the sun first appears in the Preclassic Maya period where it is shown as a four-petalled form known as the *kin*, Mayan for 'sun' or 'day'. This motif also appears on the brow of the main sun god, Kinich Ahau, of the Classic and Postclassic periods. One of the deities that form the Palenque Triad – a powerful trinity of the important city's patron gods – is also a sun god; he represents Maya kingship, drawing together the concepts of ruler and sun.

Opposite The main face represented on this flanged votive cylinder represents the sun, embellished with the Earth Monster below and an ornate headdress above, Palenque, Mexico, *c.* 690.

Eclipses were of special interest to the Maya; seven pages of tables are devoted to them in the *Dresden Codex*. By the middle of the 8th century they had worked out when eclipses were likely to occur.

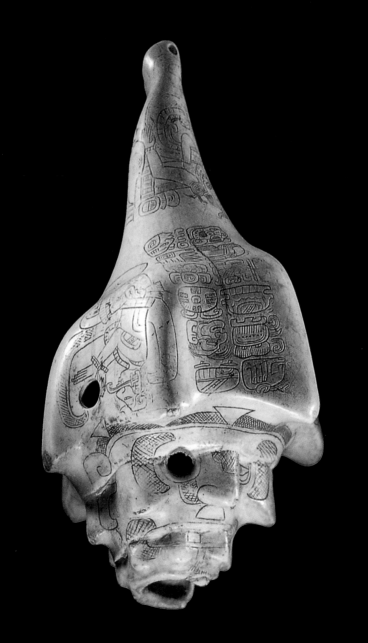

Moon

In Mayan cosmology the sun was associated with the male principle and the moon emphatically with the female. For the Maya of the Classic period the moon was represented by a beautiful goddess, usually shown sitting in the crescent of the moon, holding a rabbit. This animal, too, had a specific association with the moon, especially when full, in that its shape can be discerned in the darker areas. A legend current among the modern Maya tells how the moon's luminosity was diminished after a marital quarrel with her husband the sun in which she lost an eye.

Opposite A masterpiece of Maya art: a conch shell trumpet showing the faces of three deities, including the Jaguar Moon Lord, early Classic period, 300–500.

Venus

The Mayan Venus
had connotations
of blood and war;
when it appeared
as the Evening Star
on 29 November
735, this was taken
as the sign for two
rival cities to attack
Seibal in the Petén.

the amatory associations of the planet in Western cultures were very much alien to the Mayan view of this heavenly body, which always took the form of a male god. The Maya kept close astronomical watch on the two distinct phases of Venus as the Morning Star and the Evening Star, and the wars of the Maya of the Classic period were often timed to coincide with specific days of the planet's cycle. Hunahpu, one of the Hero Twins, shared a twin association with the sun and with Venus, as did one of the powerful gods who made up the Palenque Triad.

Opposite This leaf from the *Dresden Codex* records the movements of the planet Venus, Paris, 1810.

DIVINE BEINGS

The first publication of a Maya codex was that of five plates of the *Dresden Codex* (which the Spaniards brought to Europe in the 16th century) in Alexander von Humboldt's atlas of 1810.

Opposite This rollout view of a late Classic cylinder vase from Naranjo, Guatemala shows six gods of the Underworld.

Ritual and symbolism provided the bridges in the Maya worldview between the worlds of humans and the gods. The deities and rites of kingship were of particular importance, since they lent supernatural authority to the ruler. The gods of the Maya took various forms, often with animal attributes – such as jaguar, serpent and eagle features – and are represented in art and architecture by both pictorial and glyphic iconography.

Celestial creatures

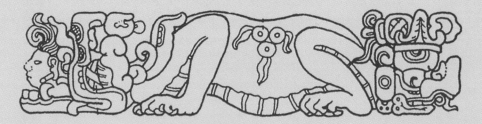

also known as the Bicephalic Monster and the Cosmic Monster, the Celestial Monster has a single body with two heads, one at each extremity, symbolizing the opposition of Venus and the sun. Sculptures of this crocodilian creature often adorned the western side of buildings, a reference to Venus leading the sun out of the Underworld. The Celestial Bird, or Principal Bird Deity, was probably based on the colourful king vulture. It was seen as evil in the *Popol Vuh*, in which its death heralds a new era of hope for the Maya.

Above The Celestial Monster in the form of an altarpiece, Copán, Guatemala.

Opposite The seventy-fourth leaf of the *Dresden Codex* shows the composite nature of the Celestial Monster: Venus, sun, sky and darkness.

Itzamna and ancient gods

In the late 19th century the scholar Paul Schellhas identified a number of gods from ancient Maya screen folds and designated each with a letter of the Latin alphabet. Of special significance were the toothless ones, who presided over Xibalba, the Underworld, Gods D, L and N. God D, with the glyphic name Itzamna ('Lizard House'), had the face of an old man, with square eyes, spiral pupils and a disc on his brow. High god of the Maya, he was often shown as a king ruling over lesser gods; he was also closely associated with the Celestial Bird. God L, also sometimes depicted with a square eye, was characterized by the muan bird headdress.

Opposite God L, seated on a bench, is attended by five young women as he watches the Hero Twins demonstrate their skill at bringing the dead back to life; painted cylinder vase, Mexico, *c.* 593–830.

Pauahtun

One of the most complex deities of the Maya pantheon, Pauahtun was a quadripartite Skybearer, appearing sometimes in a conch or turtle shell, sometimes in a spider's web.

Hunahpu, one of the Hero Twins, pulls God N from his shell before killing him; ceramic cylinder vase, Guatemala, *c.* 672–830.

Always represented with a net headdress, he was also the god of thunder and mountains, while an ancient form of Pauahtun was associated with the monkey scribes and therefore with writing and art. He is god N in the Schellhas classification of the ancient deities.

The largest human sculpture found at Copán is a colossal stone head of Pauahtun, which decorated the roof of a massive temple.

Jaguar

Maya kings and nobles dressed in a variety of jaguar garments – pelts, headdresses, even sandals and beads – to reinforce their authority.

Opposite This vase decoration shows the Water Lily Jaguar surrounded by flames as he presides over a self-decapitation.

Central to the zoomorphic symbolism of the Maya, the jaguar – king of the rainforest – was one of the most worshipped beasts of the ancient Americas, and was associated with numerous gods. The Jaguar God of the Underworld, hooked nose and knotted hair, was sometimes shown riding a great caiman from west to east; he was also the favourite motif on the shields of Maya warriors, probably because he was regarded as a god of war. The associations of the Baby Jaguar were equally sinister, since he is most often found with Chac, the god of rain and lightning, in scenes from the sacrificial death dance. His place in this central ritual is sometimes taken by the Water Lily Jaguar, so-called because of the water lily blossom or leaf on his head.

The Jester God

This intriguingly named deity had little to do with courtly mirth; the term is derived from the resemblance of his three-pointed forehead to the cap of the medieval merrymaker. The head form was almost certainly a sign of royalty translated from the three-pointed headband, which was the crown of the Maya kingship in the Preclassic period. Later, the god sometimes took the form of a shark and often appeared as a regal head ornament, made of jade. This material was the most precious mineral of the Maya, and was identified with water, sky and vegetation.

Jade enjoyed a very special status among the Maya and was the material used for some of their finest carving. Plaques and objects were widely traded between the various Maya lands during the late Classic period.

Opposite The figures of the Jester God were always carved in jade or other precious green stones; until the collapse of the Classic Maya period in the 9th century, it was also the form of the ruler's crown, 600–800.

This figure of the young Maize God once graced a temple at Copán, Honduras, c. 775. His youthful looks and the foliage surrounding his head symbolize his association with the young maize.

The Maize God

The Maize God of the early Classic period of the Maya appears as an attractive youth with maize leaves springing from the top of his head. Two later forms of the god have been identified: the Tonsured Maize God and the Foliated Maize God. The former was associated with one of the Hero Twins of the *Popol Vuh* and is so named because areas of his head appear shaved. Recently discovered murals show the god's head as ripened ears of corn, suggesting an association with the matured maize crop. The Foliated Maize God, however, has only one maize ear springing from his head and may therefore have stood for the crop during growth.

In addition to maize, the Maya also grew beans, squash, cassava and a variety of fruits. Every household had its own kitchen garden.

The paddler gods

this monstrous pair gained their name from their appearances as paddlers of the canoe of life. They were associated especially with the end of calendar periods and the blood-letting which occurred then; hieroglyphic texts give them a special relationship to the blood-letting of kings. The paddler in the bow of the canoe, Old Jaguar Paddler, represents night, while Old Stingray Paddler in the stern is the deification of day. Neither is a pretty sight: Jaguar is toothless, while Stingray has an especially aged face with a lancet, or perforator, in the septum of his nose.

Palenque Triad gods

This trio of gods only appear together in the late Classic city of Palenque. Designated GI, GII and GIII, they were all born within three weeks of each other. Two of them were identified respectively with Chac, god of rain and lightning, and with the Jaguar God of the

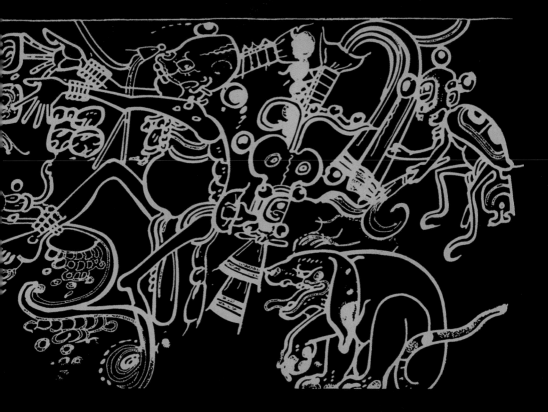

Underworld. This scene on a late Classic cylinder vessel (600–800) shows Chac dancing on the left, while Jaguar lies on the Cauac Monster, a zoomorphic mountain symbol. A third god, leg raised, extends his hands in frenzied dance.

The water bird

The oldest member of the celebrated Palenque Triad, often identified as a sun god with a particularly close association with Venus, is sometimes represented as having a water bird headdress. This symbolic creature enjoyed pre-eminent status in the mythology and symbolism of the Maya, probably reflecting the importance of the aquatic birdlife that flourished on the canals, rivers and swamps of the Maya lowlands. The bird was usually shown with a fish in its beak, which resembled that of a cormorant, although its crested head was more like that of a heron.

Opposite The handle of the lid to this early Classic tetrapod bowl (350–500) is in the form of the water bird. Its wings spread over the surface of the lid, while the cormorant-like head rears up to form the arch of the handle, completed by the fish in its beak.

The monkey scribes

Patrons of writing, art and calculations, these twins make frequent appearances in the Maya art of the Classic period. They are generally shown as being very busy with the tools of their trade: paints, books and writing brushes. Their form was often that of the howler monkey with a human body. They were also identified with the twin half-brothers of the Hero Twins in the *Popol Vuh*, Hun Batz (Howler Monkey) and Hun Chuen (Spider Monkey), who had been turned into monkeys by the mischievous Hero Twins.

The monkey scribes, both in painted and sculpted versions, were usually represented as being extremely busy with brushes and paints, as on this fine late Classic vase from Copán (*above*) or as expressed in the crouching figure (*opposite*) from the same site.

The serpent

Various monsters and beasts derived from local wildlife inhabit the Maya cosmology: rearing serpents, for instance, were central to ritual, especially to penis and tongue blood-letting. Serpents are shown rearing up to spew forth gods and ancestors. They often have two quite different heads, one at either end of a smooth or feathered body, with long snouts and even beards. The association with sacrifice was frequently reinforced by depicting the rear head as the personification of blood.

The drawing of blood from the penis took place on significant dates; the perforating instrument was a stingray spine or bone awl, usually adorned and deified.

Opposite This lintel from Chiapas, Mexico, *c.* 600–900, depicts the wife of a ruler holding the instruments of blood-letting. Above a second dish, presumably also a receptacle for blood, rises the Vision Serpent, symbol of contact with gods and ancestors.

Chac

One of the great gods of the Maya, Chac – the god of rain – is still venerated by Maya peoples today. His appurtenances were many and varied: catfish whiskers, reptilian snout, body scales and bound hair. He is frequently shown with an axe or serpent, indicating his

status as god of lightning. His connection with water and rain is often represented by showing his image in streams of falling water, the beneficial effects of which also characterized him as a patron of agriculture and provider of maize.

Opposite This pottery incense burner from Mayapan, *c.* 1200, is in the form of the rain god Chac. In one hand he carries a small bowl and in the other a ball of flaming incense.

BLOOD AND KINGSHIP

The Maya practised hereditary kingship, the succession generally passing from father to son. There is, however, evidence that two of the rulers of Palenque were women. The accession to kingship was intimately connected with blood-letting and

Below Son of Lord Pakal, the renowned ruler of Palenque, Kan-Xul accedes to the throne, his parents seated on either side of him, Palenque, Mexico, 721.

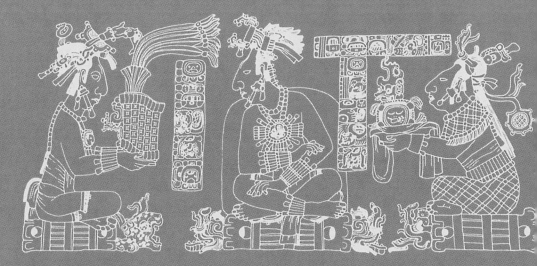

sacrifice – the release of the substance which bound Maya society together, placated the gods and set the seal of sacred authority upon the new ruler. Some surviving monuments show Maya lords seated high above prisoners prepared for sacrifice, while bloody footprints marked the steps of the king to his throne. In Classic Maya art, the king himself is often represented in the act of sprinkling blood, recalling the creation myth.

Pomp and circumstance: clay figure of a Maya ruler seated on his throne.

Strife and warfare

War, with its attendant possibilities of
capture and subsequent sacrifice,
provided a rich vein of symbolism for
the Maya, and monuments celebrating
battles are numerous. Hereditary
kingship was the customary political
system of the Maya city-states and, in
spite of family ties, it was a structure
which often led to armed
confrontation. The captives from the
vanquished side provided a ready supply
of sacrificial victims for the blood rituals
so necessary for the stability of Maya
society. Warfare in the late Classic period
became more a means of territorial
expansion than of support for a world
of symbol and ritual.

The costumes worn by the figures on this late Classic carved lintel from Piedras Negras, 667, designate them as lords (standing) and warriors (kneeling). Capes made of broad strips were worn by both groups in the Maya lands.

Lord Pakal

Unique among all Mesoamerican pyramids, the Temple of Inscriptions at Palenque was almost certainly built as a funerary monument on the orders of Pakal, one of the greatest of the city-state rulers. Pakal became king at the age of twelve and ruled until his death at eighty in 683. A series of symbols decorate the tomb and a splendid jade mosaic mask was buried with the body. The name Pakal meant literally 'hand shield' and could be written either as a picture of a shield or spelt out phonetically.

The crypt of Pakal at Palenque was finally opened in 1952; the entrance had been deliberately concealed. Inside, a great rectangular stone slab decorated with relief carvings overlaid the actual sarcophagus.

Opposite The life-sized jade and mosaic mask of Lord Pakal was found in the funerary crypt of the Temple of Inscriptions at Palenque. It was buried with the king on his death.

Palenque

Under Pakal, the city of Palenque became one of the most splendid in the whole of the Maya lands. For a period of about 150 years from 600 it expanded rapidly, with a massive building programme. The great palace probably took over a hundred years to build and was clearly intended to bring a new luxury to courtly life; great stone carvings celebrated the achievements of the rulers. The carvers of Palenque used a fine limestone to make their panels; in one, Pakal's second son who became king in 702, is shown seated between his dead parents who offer him a jade-plated headdress and shield.

The great palace of Palenque (*opposite*) yielded such treasures as this stucco head (*below*).

The court

Once a king had taken his place on the throne it was likely that he would remain in office until his death, so that he would – unless captured – be able to enjoy a lengthy court life, with all its attendant symbolism and ritual. Apart from the dimensions of sacrifice and blood-letting, there was a lighter side to life. Clowns, for instance, would have given performances in which they personified gods and demons. Court ritual also included the performance of music by singers and instrumental players equipped with an assortment of flutes, rattles, drums, gongs and conch shells.

Left This ceramic expression of the art of courtly love dates from the late Classic period. Women were quite frequently represented in Mayan art, usually as one of two archetypes: the courtly woman and the courtesan – the latter appearing with Underworld deities or even rabbits.

Court life undoubtedly had a gentler, more peaceful side; this drinking scene depicted on a late Classic vase shows a Maya dignitary admiring himself in a mirror held by a dwarf.

Costume

dress among the Maya was an
elaborate extension of social code and
symbolism. One important feature
of all accession ceremonies would
have been the ordering of new
robes for the dignitaries in
attendance. Warriors
sometimes adopted costumes made from the
pelts or feathers of potent animals or birds.
Some early Classic period representations show
the use of coyote fur, while eagle and jaguar
warriors parade at the Tula and Chichén Itzá
sites. Noble women might have worn a
cape and skirt with a mother of pearl
waist ornament, symbolizing the womb
and the Maize God, who had special
significance in Maya costume.

Opposite These
murals at Bonampak,
c. 790, depict a high-
ranking dignity in
glorious apparel,
contrasting with the
simple garments of
the attendants.

Temples and tombs

the concepts of 'temple' and 'tomb' tended to overlap in the Maya worldview. The former was often constructed, as in Pakal's Palenque, to enshrine the latter. Buildings which may very well have been closer to palaces have also attracted the term 'temple' in the past. The Maya temple proper consisted of a platform with chambers above, with access by a single staircase, also symbolizing the descent to the Underworld. In the case of the Temple of Inscriptions at Palenque, a secret staircase led down to Pakal's tomb and sarcophagus, probably the most extraordinary in the whole of Mesoamerica.

One of the wonders of Maya civilization, the 7th-century Temple of Inscriptions at Palenque was the burial site of Lord Pakal.

Captives and sacrifice

human sacrifice was a powerful, complex symbol of the binding together of men and gods in Mesoamerican societies; it was one element in social practice which truly shocked the invading Spaniards. From the evidence of late Classic depictions, the Maya generally decapitated their victims, often after torture. The sacrificial victims may have been slaves bought for the purpose or captured enemies; there is some evidence that parents even sold children for sacrifice. High-ranking members of an enemy were particularly prized as victims, since their prestige made them a more valuable offering to the gods.

Opposite Its scalp hanging from its head, body contorted in pain, mouth open in one last, dreadful scream, this late Classic figurine of a sacrificial captive encapsulates the bloody side of life.

Blood and hearts

All Mesoamerican peoples placed a special value on blood and hearts as sacrificial offerings. The blood was a symbol of man's debt to the gods who had created him; the heart, as the most vital organ, was the most precious food for the lords of creation. Much Maya sacrifice was by decapitation, but there is evidence that especially important occasions were symbolized by the removal of the heart.

The *Popol Vuh* refers to killer bats in the Underworld – a motif used to decorate the buildings in Maya cities in which captives were tortured and killed.

Heart offering (*opposite*) and ritual killing, were the means by which the Maya placated the gods and ensured continuing order in the cosmos. One such scene (*above*) shows the victim held down by four acolytes while a priest uses a flint knife to remove the heart, while a cloud serpent – the presumed recipient of the offering – watches the process.

This ball court marker was one of three at Copán, Honduras; it
portrays the players gathered around the large rubber ball.

The ballgame

the ritual exchange of
the ballgame so fascinated
the conquering Spaniards
that a troupe of players
was taken to Europe in
1528. The game was played between teams of
two to three players; points were scored by
aiming the rubber ball towards small stone
rings or markers along the sides and ends of
the court. Only the thighs and upper arms
could be used to control it. The game
probably symbolized the movement of the
sun, moon and Venus, with the ball being
seen as the sun moving in and out of the
Underworld, symbolized by the ball court.

**The ball court at
Copán is the most
perfectly preserved
of the Classic
Maya period. It is
built of stucco-
faced masonry,
with three stone
markers on either
side and three
more set into the
floor of the court.**

Overleaf A rollout view of a panoramic depiction of the
ballgame on a vase. The glyphic texts shown between
the players represent the comments of the participants.

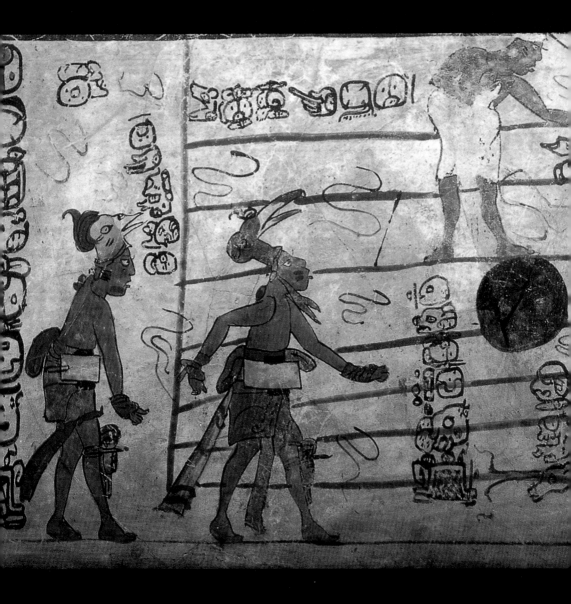

The Underworld

the best account of the ballgame and its links to the afterlife and the Underworld occurs in the *Popol Vuh*, where the Hero Twins, the greatest ballplayers in the world, outwit the gods of Xibalba, literally the 'place of fright'. This defeat of the old gods of death was something every Maya had to do to achieve regeneration and rise to the heavens, but not before journeying through a vile, decayed Underworld immediately after death. The journey was believed to be so harrowing that the deceased was buried with all manner of protective objects.

Opposite The Princeton Vase, Guatemala, *c.* 672–830, shows the defeat of the gods of the Underworld by the Hero Twins.

Religions

The Buddha

THE THREE JEWELS

The 2500-year history of Buddhism has seen its beliefs, rituals and symbolism gradually spread from its birthplace in India to Tibet, Nepal, the countries of Southeast Asia and Japan. Unlike other major religions, Buddhism

Page 326 The Buddha in the diamond posture from a *tanka* (portable religious painting), Khara Khoto, central Asia, before 1227.

Opposite Assembly tree of the gods, *tanka*, Tibet, early 19th century.

teaching in terms of this trinity, and
these Three Jewels constitute the world
of the Buddhist. The representations
of the Buddha, for instance, can
indicate many things – meditation,
teaching, enlightenment or death –
according to attitude or posture;
even the Buddha's feet have their
own particular significance.

The *dharma*, the doctrine of the
Buddha based on his formulation
of the Four Noble Truths, is
symbolized by the wheel, while
other symbols crystallize
for the initiate the
way in which the

does not have a judgmental deity at its head, but rather places the responsibility for salvation in the hands of its disciples, both lay and ordained. The latter, the monastic communities, occupy a central position in the Buddhist world; in their practices and in their art and architecture, we shall find the most complex symbolism associated with the Buddha, 'the enlightened one'. But because of the very openness of this tolerant and accommodating religion, the symbolism itself is often very subtle.

Much of it concerns the Buddha himself, his life and representations, his doctrine (*dharma*) and the community of Buddhists (*sangha*), known as 'The Three Jewels'. The Buddha saw his life and

Opposite The Buddha descending from a mountain after preaching, ink painting, China, *c.* 14th century.

teachings must be applied. Those who follow the *dharma* constitute the *sangha*, the community of Buddhists in its wider sense, but more usually applied strictly to the monastic orders which ensure the survival of the *dharma* and lives a life of devotion to the original values taught by the Buddha. These values are made manifest in both secular and monastic life by an elaborate system of symbols.

Opposite The Three Jewels: the Buddha, with begging bowl, and figures of monks, the *sangha*, by which humanity participates in the *dharma*, detail from a *tanka*, Tibet, 19th century.

THE BUDDHA

The ways of representing the figure of the Buddha through the ages often reflect the stages of his life and his teaching. Born about 566 BC in the region of Terai in Nepal to parents of the Sakya tribe, he was later known as Sakyamuni, or 'sage of the Sakya tribe', or as Gautama, his clan name. He also referred to himself as Tathagata, or 'one who follows in the path of his predecessors', although his own forename was Siddhartha, meaning 'aim attained'. Later worshippers came to know him through images and symbols, which reflected the episodes of his life and his meditation techniques.

Opposite Queen Maya gives birth to her son the Buddha through her right side in this Tibetan painting.

尔時太子出城南門見一病人問因緣時

The Three Marks of Impermanence

The first significant event in the adult life of Gautama was his encounter with the Three Marks of Impermanence: old age, illness and death. After a life of ease and privilege, during which he married and had a son and lived under the protection of his father, the Buddha strayed beyond the normal confines of the family grounds and there encountered three sights which were to transform his life: an old man, crippled by age; a man riddled with disease; and a corpse borne on its final journey to the cremation ground. Such was the young man's sense of suffering that he decided to seek true salvation.

The Buddha is said to have been told by the women of his household of the beauty of the woods beyond the house. These revelations made him especially anxious to see life beyond the confines of his family.

Opposite The life of the young Buddha: the encounters with the aged man and the sick man, silk painting, China, 8th or early 9th century.

Enlightenment

The ultimate enlightenment, the goal for Buddhists, was symbolized by the right hand reaching down to touch the earth.

$\mathbf{a}$fter failing to reach complete spiritual satisfaction through a regime of unremitting asceticism and ardent study of the teachings of others, the Buddha continued his wanderings. Eventually he found himself in Bodh Gaya, and there, sheltered by an ancient fig tree, the Bodhi Tree, he gave himself up to transcendental meditation for forty-nine days before attaining total enlightenment.

Opposite The Buddha touches the earth with his right hand, the posture of enlightenment, detail from silk painting, China, *c.* 900.

The Buddha sets in motion the wheel of the *dharma*,
relief, Afghanistan, 5th century.

In the deer park

during the period before his enlightenment beneath the fig tree, five mendicants accompanied the Buddha and witnessed his efforts to achieve the highest spiritual knowledge through asceticism. After his abandonment of that path, the five left him and repaired to the deer park near Benares, to which the Buddha returned after enlightenment. There, he delivered the discourse 'The Setting in Motion of the Wheel of the Doctrine', in which he laid down the Four Noble Truths.

Overleaf The Buddha preaching to his disciples, illuminated manuscript, Burma, 19th century.

The Buddha was especially critical of both those who placed a premium on the world of the senses, and of those who deliberately tormented themselves as a way to salvation.

Death of the Buddha

the death of Sakyamuni was no ordinary death, but rather another turn in the cycle of rebirth and suffering. It was at the age of eighty that the Buddha, accompanied by his favourite follower, Ananda, and other disciples, was finally overtaken by illness. Reclining between two trees in Kusinagara in India, he addressed his faithful band, urging them to work towards their own enlightenment, but refusing to pronounce on what happens to an enlightened person after death, since that is beyond human thought and expression.

When the Buddha reached Kusinagara, he ordered Ananda to prepare a couch for him, announcing that this was the night that he, Tathagata, would enter nirvana.

Opposite The dying Buddha reclining between the two trees of Kusinagara, *tanka*, Tibet, late 19th or early 20th century.

Images of the Buddha

about five hundred years after the death of the Buddha there began to emerge a new school of Buddhism, the Mahayana, which concentrated on the more abstract, celestial aspects of the teacher's power, in contrast to the Theravada, the 'path of the elders', which sought inspiration in the episodes of the Buddha's life on earth. Hence, the representation of the Buddha in Mahayana art, prevalent in northern Asia, tended to be as a transcendent being. The soles of the Buddha's feet and his footprints were also venerated, symbolizing the grounding of the transcendent and its application to the present.

After his death, the relics of the Buddha were the object of veneration and worship. Ambassadors were even sent from seven neighbouring kingdoms to ask for parts of them.

Opposite Offerings of petals and coins on a representation of the Buddha's footprints adjacent to the Mahabodhi Temple, Bodh Gaya.

The Buddha crowned

The images of the Buddha have, through the ages, acquired special attributes: cranial enlargement, to indicate superior mental and spiritual powers, for example, or curled and tufted hair. The Mahayana view of the regal, celestial status of the Buddha inspired some notable images, including the crowned Buddha and the Buddha with arms raised as world ruler. The first examples of the crowned figure occurred after the 7th century in India, and were then taken up in Central Asia where the Mahayana school was especially well established and much taken by the regal aspects of the sage.

Opposite The Buddha crowned – the image for those disciples of purified minds, gilded copper alloy, China, early 15th century.

The walking Buddha

this highly stylized way of representing the Buddha was closely associated with the ancient Thai capital of Sukhothai. It was characterized especially by a peculiar grace in the proportions and suggested movement of the Buddha – symbolizing, perhaps, the final harmony achieved in his life. Most standing Buddhas from other parts of Asia convey the act of walking only by the position of the head, but the images from Sukhothai show the Buddha striding forward with great balance and elegance, reminding Buddhists, perhaps, of the peripatetic, mendicant origins of the faith.

Left A rare image of the Buddha walking, bronze, Sukhothai, Thailand, 14th century.

Every aspect of physical movement – sitting, standing still, walking – should be a matter for careful consideration, according to Ashvaghosha, an Indian poet of the 1st or 2nd century AD.

The Buddha in graceful movement against the background of his throne, bronze, India, 6–7th century.

The seated Buddha

The image of the Buddha seated is the one which most suggests peace in a turbulent world. It is one, too, which is particularly appropriate to worship, although each separate effigy needs to acquire spiritual significance through consecration rituals before it becomes powerful enough to be the recipient of prayer. The image, too, once thus rendered meaningful, may also act as an inspiration to meditation in the way a mandala gives the devotee a guiding structure for spiritual reflection. Seated Buddhas in the meditation or enlightenment postures are sometimes surmounted by a parasol, symbol of the fig tree which sheltered Sakyamuni when he achieved nirvana.

According to Buddhist tradition, the great sage is always represented sitting under the Bodhi Tree as he makes his vow to seek enlightenment.

Opposite Hands in the discussion position, this Buddha is seated on a lotus, symbol of his teaching, ink on paper, China, 10th century.

The meditating Buddha

Ashvaghosha's writings on meditation advocate sitting cross-legged, preferably in a lonely place, and concentrating on the tip of the nose or the space between the eyebrows.

During the night under the fig tree the Buddha eventually gained enlightenment through meditation: on his former lives, on the birth and death of beings and on the ignorance which had held him bound to this world and to the constant necessity of rebirth. In representations of the Buddha, especially in Southeast Asia, we find the meditation posture constantly recurring. The Buddha is characteristically in a seated position, hands clasped in front of the body, with an expression of supreme calm.

Opposite The Buddha in the meditation posture, gilt statue, Bangkok, Thailand, 14th century.

The celestial cosmic Buddha

the Mahayana school of Buddhism, which emerged about five hundred years after the death of Sakyamuni, placed fresh emphasis on the whole pantheon of Buddhas and bodhisattvas. This emphasis is even more striking in esoteric Buddhism – Indian and Tibetan Tantrism, for instance – where the

This scroll, depicting a series of Buddhas under different names, was used in ceremonies on the last day of the lunar year, ink and colours on paper, China, 10th century.

gods are divided into five main groups, each
under one of five celestial Buddhas and each
divided into quarters. This five/four symbolism
is extended to make the great cosmic diagrams in
the form of mandalas. The Buddha's universality
was celebrated in the legend that he could
assume a thousand forms.

Bodhisattvas

Literally 'enlightened being', from *sattva*, 'being' or 'essence', and *bodhi*, the 'wisdom arising from the realization of the ultimate truth', the bodhisattva played a crucial role in Mahayana Buddhism. The ideal of the bodhisattva was to renounce nirvana in order to help all other beings to salvation. These figures are often shown richly attired, emphasizing their worldliness in contrast to the simplicity of the Buddha. Important bodhisattvas often depicted include Maitreya, the Buddha to be, crowned by a dome-shape called a *stupa*; Vajrapani, the protector of Buddha, holding a thunderbolt; and Avalokiteshvara, the embodiment of compassion, protecting travellers.

Opposite The bodhisattva Avalokiteshvara as a guide, ink and colours on silk, China, 10th century.

Nagarjuna, an influential Indian Buddhist thinker of the 3rd century, described a bodhisattva as someone destined to become a Buddha.

Goddesses

female deities had traditionally acted as symbols of fertility in early Indian religions. In Buddhism such figures were known as *yakshinis*. The growth of Tantric Buddhism, an esoteric body of beliefs and practices, saw a considerable increase in the number and complexity of female figures. Some of these were multi-limbed monsters, expressive of great evil, while others symbolized wisdom and were presented in passive, beatific postures.

The meaning of the goddess Tara is one of the hardest to unravel in the Tibetan Buddhist pantheon; she has as many heads and legs as she has arms, a complex arrangement which may account for the rarity of such sculptures.

Opposite Tara is Avalokiteshvara's female counterpart; she is the scourge of humans, birds and animals. The two cubes beneath her feet symbolize egocentric existence, partly gilt brass, Tibeto-Chinese, 18th century.

DHARMA

After achieving enlightenment under the Bodhi Tree, the Buddha continued his meditations, formulating a doctrine, which could then be passed on to others. This doctrine became known as the *dharma*, meaning 'law' or 'teaching'. It was said to have first been recited after the death of the Buddha by the disciple Ananda, and it then became the guiding principle for the whole community of Buddhists. Central to the doctrine are the Four Noble Truths, though the teaching of Buddhism has never been rigid and doctrinaire; it has always adapted to circumstances. Certain symbols and emblems, however, retain enduring significance, such as the wheel and the path.

Opposite The translation of Buddhist scripture into Tibetan: here the translator, watched over by Buddhas and bodhisattvas, hands down leaves to copying scribes, *tanka*, Tibet, 18th century.

The Four Noble Truths

EVERYTHING IS SUFFERING.

THE ORIGIN OF SUFFERING IS DESIRE.

THERE EXISTS NIRVANA, AN END TO SUFFERING.

A PATH, DEFINED BY THE BUDDHA, LEADS TO NIRVANA.

Opposite The Wheel of Life illustrates *samsara*, the ongoing cycle of birth, life and death, one of the most important concepts of Buddhist doctrine, gouache on cloth, Tibet, 18th century.

these four truths were the central points of the Buddha's doctrine. The first refers to the unsatisfactory nature of life and its impermanence. Our belief in selfhood is the second truth: self has five components or *skandhas* – matter, sensation, perception, mental formation and consciousness. Nirvana is the end of suffering, the abandonment of selfhood. Finally, there is The Noble Eightfold Path, which leads to the end of suffering: right understanding, right thought, right speech, right action, right livelihood, right effort, right mindfulness and right meditation.

The wheel

From earliest times Buddhist art was characterized by rich symbolism, often derived from the Buddha's first teachings. Images of trees, thrones and wheels were especially significant. The wheel was an emblem of the *dharma*, the setting in motion of the wheel of law, and therefore a symbol of the Buddha himself. It could also be symbolized by the circle formed by bringing the tips of thumb and forefinger together, signifying the perfection which is neither beginning nor end.

Opposite Symbol of the *dharma*, the wheel became one of the most elaborately worked symbols of Buddhist iconography, low-relief sculpture in silver-gilt, copper and semi-precious stones, Tibet, 19th century.

The path

The fourth Noble Truth of the Buddha's doctrine refers to the path towards enlightenment, nirvana. Later teaching divided the path into stages – from morality to meditation, and then to wisdom. The Buddha, however, recognized that wholehearted commitment to following the path was virtually impossible for anyone living in the world of normal human exchange and therefore propounded his doctrine of the 'Middle Way' between luxury and asceticism. Meditation walks, terminating in a shelter housing the image of a skeleton, are still used by monks in Sri Lanka to represent the path of earthly life.

Opposite The stages along the path to enlightenment are illustrated by the progression of an elephant who gradually turns from black to white in this mural from the Likir monastery, Ladakh, India.

The Buddha, quoted by Ashvaghosha in the *Buddhacarita*, saw the way to supreme enlightenment as a path trodden for the sake of all that is sad in the world.

The Bodhi Tree

this central symbol in Buddhist iconography represents the original fig tree which sheltered the Buddha during the extraordinary night of his enlightenment. In early Buddhist art the figure of the Buddha in the enlightenment posture was often shown with cuttings from the fig tree, later stylized as the royal parasol, symbol of the shelter given him by the tree during his night of liberation. Cuttings from the fig tree were taken to bless any new site devoted to the religion. In later, more elaborate monastic structures, the tree was symbolized in the crowning finial of the *stupa*.

Opposite Painting on a leaf showing a monkey offering a peach (symbol of sexual enjoyment) to a devotee beneath a *bodhi* tree, China, 19th century.

Posture

Just as representations of the Buddha show him in various postures to symbolize certain states – meditation, enlightenment, leadership and death – so posture and position are used as aids to the successful negotiating of the path to enlightenment. Buddhist statuary almost always suggests grace and ease, as though expressing the spirituality of the subject. In Zen Buddhism the process of awakening is helped by the technique of *zazen*, in which the initiate sits cross-legged in the lotus position and brings his mind to a state of peace and tranquillity by slow, rhythmic breathing.

Below Buddhist statuary is characterized by postures of great physical gracefulness, as in this figure of a listening disciple, Burma, 19th century.

Opposite A more regal figure is this bodhisattva, polychromed wood, China, 12th–13th century.

Hands

In Buddhism, as in Hinduism, movements of the hands are seen to symbolize movements of the mind and, as such, are central to expressing the meaning of the *dharma*. Many of these hand gestures (*mudra*) may be observed in representations of the Buddha. To the initiate the vocabulary is very clear: thumb and forefinger closed recall the wheel, and therefore the *dharma* itself; the hands upright and open signify the teaching of the doctrine; the open hand pointing downwards is the gesture of generosity and giving; hands folded on the lap indicate meditation.

Opposite The hands of a monk in the wheel gesture, Eiheiji Temple, Fukui, Japan.

Lotus

Spiritual purity, *bodhi*, is symbolized especially by the eight-petalled white lotus, the lotus of the Buddha.

Opposite This lotus, symbol of the *dharma*, rises up to the heavens to support the figure of a monk, symbol of the *sangha*, detail from a *tanka*, Tibet, 19th century.

The aquatic lotus was an ideal symbol of the progress of the soul: its roots grow in muddy waters, representative of human desires, while the leaves and flowers open up to the sun, to enlightenment. Legends of the Buddha's childhood tell how the infant caused a lotus to spring up every time his foot touched the ground as he took his first steps. The opening of the lotus also symbolizes the opening of the *chakras*, the nerve centres of the body.

Mandala

A mandala can assume any size: the largest one in the world is the temple complex of Borobudur, Java, a colossal edifice of concentric terraces and *stupas*.

Opposite Mandala with Buddha and bodhisattvas, ink on silk, Japan, *c.* 859–880.

as an aid to spiritual fulfilment and, therefore, to progress along the path to enlightenment, the mandala is a central emblem of Buddhism. Its circular form – with neither beginning nor end – and concentric structure reflect the shape of the universe outside and the sense of perfection within. Buddhist mandalas guide meditation and prayer and also often reflect the forms of the cosmos. At the centre of the universe – both physical and spiritual – is Mount Meru, surrounded by seven concentric mountain ranges separated by the seven oceans. Beyond the outermost range lie the great ocean and the four island continents, including the southernmost, Jambudvipa, the home of humans. In the heights of Mount Meru live the four Buddhas of the cardinal points and, at its peak, the celestial Buddha, Vairochana.

Meditation

The Buddha taught that the way to enlightenment is through meditation and the achievement of a calm, clear state of being, mirroring his own experience under the Bodhi Tree. This discipline of constructive thought will enable the disciple to rise above the forces of ignorance, desire and hatred, which make up the continuous cycle of suffering, *samsara*. In Zen Buddhism the meditation discipline of *zazen* has two characteristics: stopping (*shi*) and view (*kan*).

Opposite A monk of a Japanese Buddhist sect sits in meditation beneath a tree, savouring the delights of nature as an aid to gaining true spirituality, Japan, 12th–13th century.

Light

The light of the world rising up through the *chakras* leads to the supreme enlightenment. Light is everywhere in the universe in various shades and intensities and is therefore a symbol of the ultimate reality and always one of the main offerings at Buddhist shrines. In Thailand this may take the form of an orange candle combined with flowers and three sticks of sandalwood. The first symbolizes individual consciousness; the second, the senses; and the third, the tripartite division of Buddhism, the Three Jewels of Buddha, *dharma* and *sangha*. Valuable materials, such as butter, are used to make candles, signifying the importance of the offering.

In Buddhism light is particularly associated with the positive aspects of life after death, guiding the departed one to various worlds of delight.

Opposite Butter lamps, Dharamsala, India.

Water

Like the light of the candle, water is a frequent symbolic offering at Buddhist shrines and temples. It is closely associated with the symbolism of the moon as an image of the feminine, regenerative power in the universe. On special occasions and for particular deities the water may be further purified by the addition of herbs. Contemplation of water, whether still or falling, is also regarded as an aid to meditation. In Zen Buddhism especially, the initiate will go through several levels of consciousness to reach a true appreciation of the very essence of the substance.

A tranquil lake is a metaphor in Zen for a mind, which has become pure and calm through meditation.

Opposite Water has long been recognized as an aid to meditation; here, in this Chinese temple, its tranquillity makes an apt setting for the symbolic *stupa*.

The serpent

Ashvaghosha described the cross-legged posture adopted by the Buddha in meditation as making the legs 'massive like the coils of a sleeping serpent'.

Opposite The Buddha is sheltered by the serpent-being Muchalinda, who had protected him during a storm in the garden at Bodh Gaya, Cambodia, 12th century.

The serpent Kundalini in Tantric symbolism represents the force rising up through the body, opening up the *chakras* until it reaches the seventh *chakra* of the 'thousand-petalled' lotus, positioned just above the head. Always an object of veneration in the animistic cultures of Southeast Asia, the serpent was assimilated into the body of Buddhist belief as a protective presence, especially of the teachings and temples. As water symbols, serpents were seen as links between heaven and earth and often appeared as sculptural decoration in temple architecture – on bridges, over water, or at entrances to temple complexes – to symbolize the passage from one state to another.

SANGHA

The third jewel of Buddhist belief is the *sangha* – the community of those who have accepted the tenets of the *dharma*. In its broadest sense the *sangha* is four-fold, including monks, nuns, laymen and laywomen; the former two categories are distinguished from the latter by dress, way of life and intensity of spiritual application. All members of the *sangha* aspire to enlightenment, as taught by the Buddha.

Left Marble statue of a monk with begging bowl, Burma, 19th century; villagers, however poor, are expected to help sustain Buddhist communities by giving to the monks (*opposite*), illuminated manuscript, Thailand, 19th century.

Pillars

Visual symbolism in the holy places
of Buddhism only began to appear
approximately three hundred years after
the Buddha's death. In northern India,
the Emperor Ashoka (ruled *c.* 273–232 BC),
a convert to Buddhism, took over the
practice of pillar worship from earlier
Indian cults to promote the spread of
Buddhism. Pillars in stone and wood,
carved with the sayings of the Buddha and
surmounted by symbolic beasts, were set
up throughout the empire, from Bengal
to Afghanistan, recalling the memorial
columns of Mesopotamia.

Left The most famous pillar of Emperor Ashoka is
the lion in polished sandstone at Sarnath, India.

Stupa

After the relics of the Buddha had been dispersed to various kingdoms, the rulers erected *stupas* in their principal cities to house them.

the best known of all Buddhist monuments, the *stupa* is formed of a dome with a pillar emerging from its top. It is a simple icon of the Buddha's conquest of the world of illusion and his attainment of nirvana. The pillar itself represents the *axis mundi*, the pivotal point of the earth, the mystical Mount Meru, and is often enclosed by three umbrellas, symbolizing the Three Jewels. Circumambulation of the *stupa* is seen as an aid to meditation.

Overleaf A Nepalese monastery consisting of just four cells and *stupa*, illuminated manuscript, Nepal, AD 1015.

यापद्माद्दन
नाल्विोसाद
नसमायत्र
यामेयवाम
स्वामहास्क्क
रास्लिनवाय
१२

Temple of the universe

buddhist temples are themselves symbols of great complexity. They are, in effect, four-dimensional maps of the universe according to the Buddhist cosmology. In Thai temples, for instance, there is a dominating central tower, a reference to Mount Meru, the sacred mountain and central axis of the cosmos, from which other elements of the complex are laid out according to the cardinal directions. The domed form of the *stupa* has a symbolic role in both time and space as a reference to the Cosmic Egg, the origin of the universe. Indeed, every level of the *stupa* is rich in symbolism: the base, dome, spire, capital and finial are associated with, respectively, earth, water, fire, air and ether – the five elements.

Opposite Samye, the oldest Buddhist teaching monastery in Tibet, a symbolic model of the cosmos built on the diagram of the mandala, gouache on a cotton *tanka*, Tibet, 18th–19th century.

Shrines and sanctuaries

as expressions of the monastic, meditational aspects of Buddhism, sanctuaries and pilgrim shrines were associated with the very early periods of religion. The need for peace and quiet for constructive reflection gave such plans a central role, both practical and symbolic, in the development of Buddhism. Particularly notable are the rock sanctuaries of western India, often embellished with wood, a reminder of the early days spent by the Buddha and his followers in the forest. Pilgrims gather in temple relic *stupas* for worship.

Ashvaghosha in the *Saundaranandakavya* prophesies a longer life, strength and the ability to eliminate faults as the result of solitary meditation.

Shrines and holy places were sometimes taken over from local religions; this 14th-century Shinto mandala *(opposite)* from Kumano, Japan shows the gods as Buddhas and bodhisattvas. Monks' cells *(left)* are also regarded as places of intense spirituality.

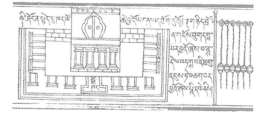

Entrances

as holy buildings, especially those containing images of the Buddha, are symbols of the highest spiritual attainment, so the entrances to them are of particular significance. Symbols of the transition to a higher plane of being, temples and *stupas* are often embellished with massively elaborate decoration, emphasizing the importance to the initiate of the act of entering the shrine. Doors, too, may be richly carved, reflecting to the outside world the intensely sacred nature of the shrine's interior. The theme of passing from exterior to interior and vice versa is taken up again in bridges and their balustrades.

In the cave temples of Ellora, India, bodhisattvas guard the preaching Buddha in a doorway carved in solid rock, 5th–10th century.

Teacher and pupil

Just as entrances and bridges symbolize the passing from one spiritual state to another, so the relationship of teacher and pupil within the *sangha* is one in which the changing states of consciousness are of paramount importance. Although there are certain communal activities which give structure to monastery life, it is the passing on of spiritual knowledge – meditation techniques and an appreciation of the higher wisdoms – which ensures the continuing vigour of the religion. Every detail of a monk's life is redolent with symbolic meaning, and deviation from the daily round will entail a penance.

The Buddhist monk should struggle day and night to a point where he feels no weariness; then he will be ready to achieve nirvana.

Opposite An aged monk imparts wisdom to his pupils under the benevolent eye of a celestial being, wall painting, China, 9th–10th century.

An offering of
music, a medium
reflecting the
deepest rhythms of
the universe: a
graceful goddess
depicted in a fresco
in the temple of
Drepung, Lhasa,
Tibet.

Nirvana

All the symbolism associated with the *sangha* is devoted to one goal – the achievement of a state of tranquillity beyond self and the physical sense. The making of music and the intoning of mantras is seen as one of many ways of aiding communication with the gods, themselves sometimes symbolized as centres of subtle sound, and of awakening the *chakras*, the nerve centres of the body. Other activities – gardening, writing, flower arranging, for example – also help the devoted aspirant to concentrate his mind towards spiritual realization and the final silence which is enlightenment, the full assimilation of all the symbolism of the Three Jewels.

圖 胎 出

The Tao

THE LAND OF
THREE RELIGIONS

In pre-Communist China three great religions flourished, or perhaps it would be more true to term them as two religions and one way of life. The first was Confucianism, an austere and elitist body of belief of particular appeal to the Mandarin classes. Buddhism was the second, practised in many varieties by a multitude of sects. In some instances it had become little more than a system of popular magic; in this aspect it tended to overlap with some of the simpler forms of Taoism, the third great system of belief and experience. Taoism is not a set system with a central god, but a way of guidance for men and women.

Page 404 A silk canopy with dragons, symbols of celestial *yang* essences, China, 16th–17th century.

Right Lao Tzu and Confucius take care of the future Buddha, Sakyamuni, depicted as a child, silk painting, China, 14th century.

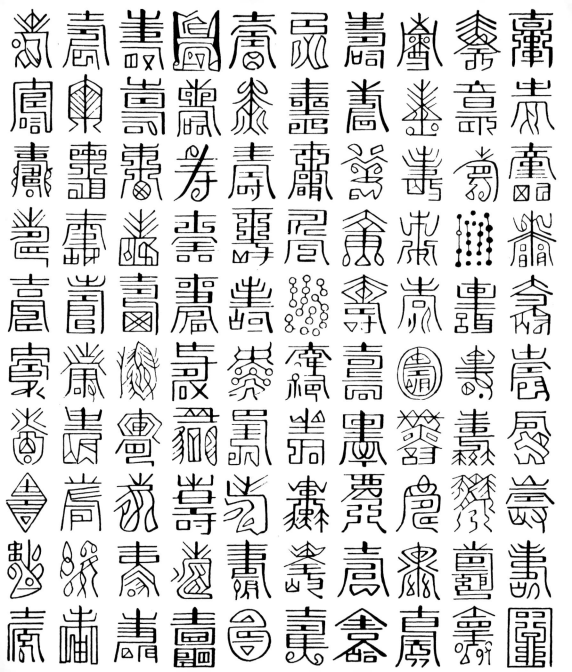

ONE PICTURE IS WORTH A THOUSAND WORDS

Taoism is rooted in symbolism; the very characters of the Chinese language are themselves potent symbols, which may also reflect the individual spirit of the writer. Calligraphy itself – the movement of the brush across the paper – symbolizes the flow of vital currents through the universe, the threads of linear continuity, which the Taoist perceives as the energizing elements of the cosmos. Secret scripts of great beauty have been developed by Taoists to express the working forces of heaven and earth both by reference and meaning and also through the form of the characters.

Above The character *shou* (longevity) has great significance in Taoism, which focuses upon the current life as opposed to an afterlife, rubbing, China, 19th century.
Opposite One hundred talismanic forms of the character *shou*.

TAO

The word 'Tao' defies translation and complete definition. According to one ancient inscription, it is 'the ancestor of all doctrines, the mystery beyond mysteries'. Sometimes inadequately rendered in English as 'the way', the Tao informs all phenomena, but can only be seen symbolically – through the flowing of water, the sexual act, the awakening of the psychic centres of the body, and valleys and mountains, where the ideal Taoist may dwell in communion with the heavens.

The Taoist adept holds open a scroll prominently embellished with the *yin/yang* symbol, silk panel, China, Ming Dynasty, 14th–17th century.

The three profound studies

Taoism's deepest principles are those of openness and accommodation, reflected in the non-doctrinal nature of the basic texts, the three great works: the *Tao Te Ching*, the *Chuang Tzu* and the *I Ching*. Through allusion and suggestion, the first introduces the Tao, the way to harmony. The *Chuang Tzu* goes further in resolving the position of man in relation to the natural world. The *I Ching* (Book of Change) is a practical oracle book, a list of possibilities, but never a work of definite instruction.

Opposite The great works of Taoism advise one seeking knowledge and harmony to identify the vital energies of the universe, represented as a three-dimensional landscape on this bronze jar (China, Western Han Dynasty, 209–206 BC) and as never-ending flow on a celadon dish (*left*), China, Ming Dynasty, 14th century.

The Tao which can be described cannot be the true Tao, which is nameless.

Lao Tzu

Lao Tzu and the Tao Te Ching

The basic document of Taoist thought, the *Tao Te Ching*, is one of remarkable shortness; compared with the lengthy texts of most of the world's systems of belief, it is a work of great compression. The short fragments of which it is composed are pieces of great subtlety and complexity, relying more on suggestion than description and asking more questions than providing answers. Sometimes known as 'The Book of Five Thousand Characters', it is generally attributed to Lao Tzu, a Chinese sage thought to be a contemporary of Confucius living in the 6th century BC. The work acquired book form around the 4th century BC.

Opposite A 10th-century rock carving of Lao Tzu, Fujian, China. He was also often shown on a water buffalo, symbolizing his flight from corruption (*below*), bronze statuette, China, Ming Dynasty, 17th century.

The hsien

The immortals of Taoism were, in many ways, ordinary beings writ large. Their power was derived not so much from innate divinity as from observing the correct way in all things and thus arriving at superhuman understanding and – often – immortality. Although some were believed to ride through the air on cranes and dragons to join the heavenly imperial court, the majority about whom the ancient stories were told lived on earth on such symbolically charged substances as cinnabar and fungus, thereby partaking of the universal energies of *yang* and *yin*.

Above Winged dragons and *hsien*, denoting closeness to the heavens, bas-relief, China, Han Dynasty, 3rd century BC–AD 3rd century.

Opposite 'Red Robe', a papier-maché figure, one of six to twelve which line the Path to Heaven in the Taoist ritual of Presenting the Memorial to the Jade Emperor, southern Taiwan.

Shou Lao

Many of the *hsien* are associated with the most potent symbolism of the Tao. Almost every association carries rich significance in the delicate balancing of inner and outer forces and influences. Shou Lao, god of longevity, was the personification of maleness and of the *yang* essences. He was therefore often associated with the dragon and the crane, symbols of long life attained by well-controlled sexual and meditational lives. Some representations show the immortal holding a peach, a *yin* symbol whose cleft was seen to be evocative of the female vulva.

Longevity is associated in the *Tao Te Ching* with suppleness and non-action, pliancy and fragility, in contrast to hardness and boldness which result in death.

The bald-headed god of longevity, Shou Lao, one of the most eminent of male *hsien*, holds up a scripture scroll and a peach, symbol of the long life, painting on paper, China, Ch'ing Dynasty, 17th–20th century.

Legendary Queen Mother of the West, symbolic figure of *yin* energies, the *hsien* Hsi Wang Mu is represented in this 16th-century Chinese silk painting with a phoenix.

Hsi Wang Mu

Although the figure of Shou Lao shows closeness to *yin* energies in his bearing of the peach, it seems appropriate that his undoubted *yang* potency should be counterbalanced by Hsi Wang Mu, 'Queen Mother of the West', who is the personification of the female *yin*, and reigns as queen of the immortals. She lives in a lush garden filled with flowers and birds where she keeps careful watch over a peach tree, upon which grows the rare peach of immortality. Hsi Wang Mu may very well be shown carrying an offering dish, symbol of female sexuality, and has served as a strong female model for Taoist adepts for centuries.

Goddesses have always played an important role in Taoism, and have been worshipped by men as well as women.

Secret harmonies

The aim of Taoism, whether in life or art, is harmony, expressed in the tales of the immortals, of saintly lives lived in mountain sanctuaries or among a celestial bestiary, as well as through the thoughtful conduct of the everyday. The emblems and iconography of traditional Chinese art are symbols of a balancing of forces, of the *yang* and the *yin*, observation of which will itself induce feelings of contentment. In the widest sense there is the balance to be sought between the fundamental ebb and flow of the universe, the male and female principles, and the forms of permanence and change.

Right The unity of all things – heaven, earth and man – is symbolized in this bowl (*yin*) decorated with penis forms (*yang*), China, Ming Dynasty, 16th century. Similar unity is expressed in the trigrams of the *pi* disc (*above*): heaven, wave and rocks are crossed by the shaft symbolizing earth, China, Ming Dynasty, 15th–16th century.

YIN YANG

The principle of polarity is at the heart of Taoist thought. Yet this emphasis on opposites must not be mistaken for a situation of conflict – everything implies its opposite, and indeed is only meaningful because the opposite is there. And so life and death, light and darkness, good and evil, positive and negative, ebb and flow, and male and female coexist as parts of one and the same system. The elimination of either half would also mean the disappearance of the other.

Something and nothing produce each other.

Lao Tzu

A painted panel with the *yin/yang* symbol surrounded by trigrams
made up of *yin* (broken) and *yang* (whole) lines.

血湖地獄燈圖　　九宮八卦土燈圖　　火德燈圖　　九天玉樞燈圖

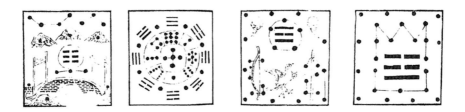

I Ching

Of the three great texts the *I Ching* comes closest to being a manual for the Taoist. Its origins are shrouded in mystery and, although thought to be of great antiquity, it is mentioned by neither Lao Tzu nor Chuang Tzu and probably originated as a body of orally transmitted folk wisdom. It differs from all other oracular texts in regarding the past, present and future as a dynamic entity, flowing and changing and therefore not

The gate of the heaven which comes after the beginning of time, in a contemporary Taoist temple (*opposite above*); the trigrams which surround it represent new energy entering the world. The continued interaction of *yin* and *yang* is represented in trigrammatic form (*opposite below* and *above*).

susceptible to strict instruction or law-making. The permutations of the *yin* and *yang* forces are worked out in terms of sixty-four hexagrams, each composed of two trigrams made up of broken (*yin*) and unbroken (*yang*) lines.

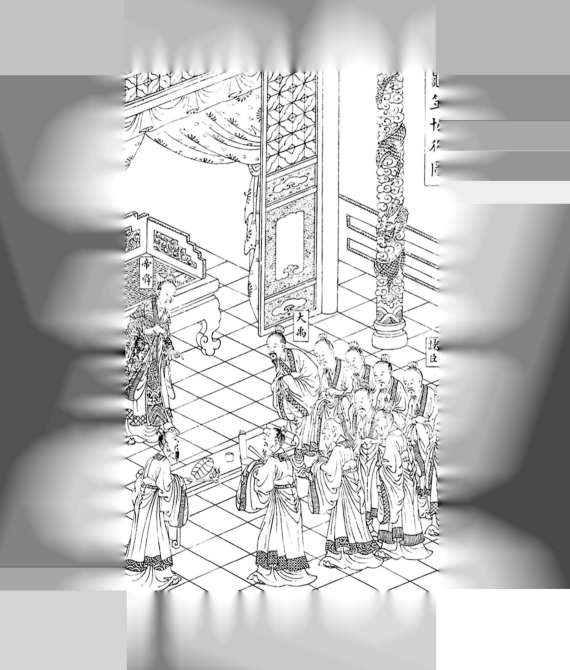

Consulting the oracle

The use of magic diagrams to obtain guidance is a practice central to Taoism; here, the Emperor prepares to divine the future by means of yarrow stalks (*opposite*). Other diagrams may be made up of randomly assorted objects or formally arranged trigrams (*above*).

the *I Ching* may be consulted in three ways; the most venerated is the fifty sticks technique, but six wands or six coins may be used. The book itself should be placed on a table free from other objects and laid on a clean piece of cloth. In Taoism it is believed that the source of wisdom lies in the north and the table should therefore be positioned in the northernmost part of the room and approached from the south; an incense burner may be placed by the sticks, wands or coins. The question to be asked should be seriously held in mind, and the outcome of tossing the sticks or coins will determine the lines of two trigrams, leading to the relevant text.

Colour and design

The polarities of *yin* and *yang* are the articulating principles of traditional Chinese art. Constant interaction of the two provides the meaning of countless paintings, wall hangings and designs on clothing and even on domestic pottery. The juxtaposition of certain colours expresses the balance of essential forces through a *yang/yin* pairing: red/blue, red/green, white/black, gold/silver. Certain types of artefact, perhaps more closely associated with a single sex, may express one force more strongly; porcelain and soapstone are more strongly identified with the female side of the household and are therefore decorated with *yin* symbols, such as baskets and fungus.

Opposite An unusual silk panel woven in contrasting colours with a phoenix and crane design, China, Ming Dynasty, 15th century.

Cosmos

Taoism is underwritten by the sense of the cyclical, by a worldview that sees everything in relation to everything else. There can be no 'before' unless there is an 'after'; in the words of Lao Tzu: 'From Tao arises one; from one arises two; from two arises three; and from three arise the ten thousand things.' The symbolic representations of the world therefore balance the *yin/yang* forces: east may be symbolized by a green dragon (*yang* rising), south by a phoenix (*yang* at its height), west by a white tiger (*yin* rising), and north by a tortoise entwined with a serpent (*yin* dominant).

Opposite The animal figures of this 17th-century Chinese mirror symbolize the unity of the Taoist cosmos.

Below This 19th-century Japanese bronze of entwined tortoise and serpent (*yin*), also has the attributes of dragon and tiger (*yang*).

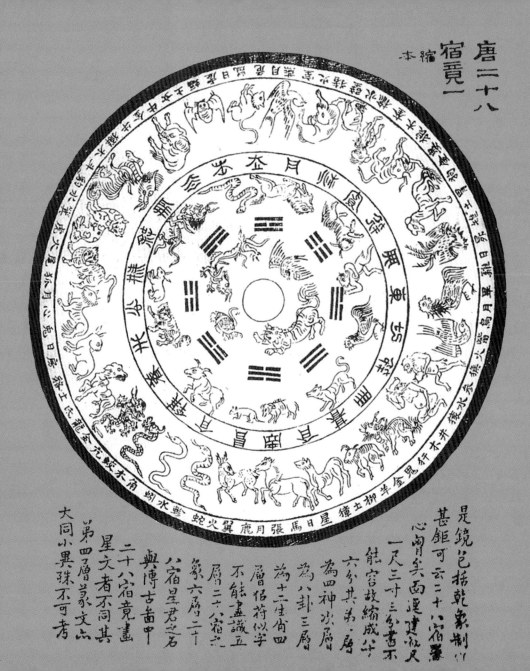

是鏡包括乾象制
甚鉅可云二十八宿鏡
心宿冐尖面邊建拔尺
一尺三十三分畫不
能容故縮成寸
六分共弟二層
為四神次層
為八卦三層
為十二生肖四
層恰符似字
不能盡識五
層二十八宿六
象六層二十
八宿星君之名
與博古畫中
二十八宿竟畫
星文者不同其
第四層蒙文亦
大同小異殊不可考

Cosmic energy is symbolized by the pearl, pursued by a blue (*yin*) dragon
against a red (*yang*) background, silk panel, Chinese, 16th–17th century.

Heaven diminishes where there is abundance, and supplements where there is deficiency.

Lao Tzu

The jade heavens

heaven and earth are themselves symbols of the *yin/yang* polarity. Inertness and receptivity are perceived as earthly *yin* characteristics, while the heavens are the concentration of vital *yang* energies. The symbolism even extended to traditional Chinese coinage – the circle (heaven) pierced by the square (earth); the circle symbolism for heaven was repeated in the *pi* disc which, like many other amulets, was often made of jade. Other stones were regarded as essence of earth, but jade, the semen of celestial dragons, was essence of heaven.

Opposite A *pi* disc made of jade decorated with embossed points to symbolize the constellations, China, *c.* 3rd century BC.

Movements of the heavens were of constant fascination to the early Taoist; in this Han Dynasty relief (*below*) an officer of the court of Ursa Major sits in a chariot, symbolizing the constellation, accompanied by phoenix and dragon.

The five earthly elements

although the mutual interdependence of the elements of the universe is expressed as *yin* and *yang*, early Taoism also expressed the cyclical nature of the world in terms of the Five Elements: wood, fire, earth, metal and water. According to the teaching of Tsou Yen (*c.* 350–270 BC), a scholar from northeast China, wood gives rise to fire, from which ash gives rise to earth, from whose depths is mined metal, whose polished surface may attract dew (water), which causes wood to grow and thus completes the cycle.

Opposite A peach-shaped box decorated with a variety of lucky emblems to signify the harmony of the universe, China, Ch'ing Dynasty, 18th century.

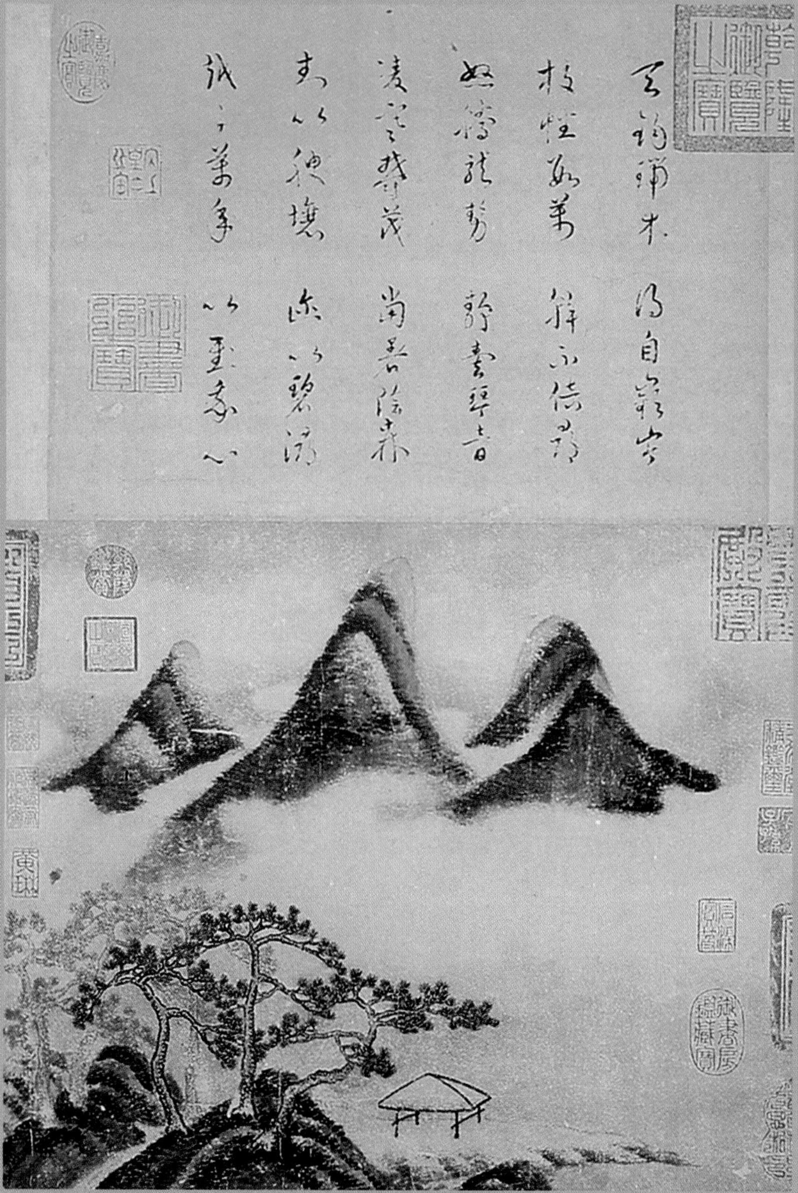

The landscape of harmony

The Tao is the essential course of nature; it is the way things are, the universal principle of order. It is expressed in the combination of natural phenomena – the relationship of mountains and valleys, of land and water, height and depth, convex and concave forms. In landscape painting, the Taoist artist will try to convey the harmonies in his subject by picking out the subtle connections between the shapes of earth formations. Mountains may be shown marked by 'dragon veins', currents of *yang* energy running through the otherwise inert *yin* of the earth.

Above A talismanic symbol represents the five great mountain peaks, the source of the five elements.

Opposite Spring Mountains and Pine Trees is a supremely harmonious painting by Mi Fei (1051–1107).

Left In Front of the Waterfall by Ma Lin shows sages contemplating a waterfall, while the climbing tree symbolizes the tenacity of the scholars, ink on silk, *c.* 1246.

Opposite A wooden stand is intricately carved with waves, China, Ch'ing Dynasty, 1769.

Water is identified in the *Tao Te Ching* as being the element closest to the highest good: it does not contend with the many creatures and plants which it nourishes, and it flows into places where no being would wish to be. In these qualities it comes close to being a complete symbol of the Tao. It is submissive and weak, yet it can successfully attack what is strong and hard.

The good of water

although the Tao is the order of the universe, it is a
very different order from the rigid concepts of Western
culture. This organic order is most perfectly symbolized
by water, the weakest element yet the strongest: 'It is
thus that Tao in the world is like a river going down the
valley to the ocean' (Lao Tzu). It takes the form of
clouds and mist, very breath of the *yin* earth, and returns
as rain, bringing *yang* energy to fill the rivers and oceans,
finding the lines of flow in the landscape. The way it
moves is a potent symbol of the vital patterns of the
universe; the way it stands still expresses peace and
understanding.

The veins in the stone

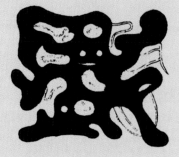

the swirling, unpredictable flow of energy so clearly seen in water is recognized by the Taoist adept in many other forms, for instance in smoke and incense rising. Such forceful veins are also reproduced in much Chinese ceramic and metalware in the form of marbling or streaking, or in the arrangement of coloured blotches. The true Taoist will find greatest satisfaction in the streaking or veining of rocks and stones, perhaps themselves worn and pitted by the steady erosion of water. Stones shaped by water have the true quality of the Tao; their irregularities suggest the interpenetration of *yang* and *yin* and, as such, are eagerly collected by the adept.

Above This diagram from the Han Dynasty, 2nd century BC, symbolizes the cavities (*yin*) in a rock (*yang*).

Opposite The deep and shallow grooves woven together in a block of wood are also evidence of veining, as in this woodcut illustrating the 9th-century love story of Ts'ui Ying-ying.

歘火會雷廷大煞雷電大作折樹誅妖孽兩傾盡

Cinnabar

Jade and cinnabar stand out in the Taoist symbolism of substances. Jade is closely associated with the celestial dragon and, therefore, with *yang* forces. But cinnabar is an even more potent symbol, expressing nothing less than the joining of *yin* and *yang*. Composed largely of sulphide of mercury, it provides red pigment for painting, but in Taoist magic it was regarded – sometimes too literally – as the elixir of life. In the inner alchemy of Taoism it came to represent the achieving of the ultimate spiritual state, the awakening of all the subtle energies of the body to bring the devotee into the most perfect harmony with the universe.

Opposite A valued and highly symbolic pigment, cinnabar is here combined with ink to illustrate the combination of fire and cloud in a Taoist almanac, China, 19th century.

Flowers and fruit

the softer, more yielding character of plant life and its obviously close dependence on the earth gives it especially strong *yin* associations. Examples would be used in Chinese art to symbolize the female element in the balance of harmonies in the whole composition. Flower decoration, for instance, might be used on tableware so that *yin* qualities would be absorbed by the food served on it. A garden of peony flowers, the setting for an intimate domestic scene, might be counterbalanced by the swooping form of a *feng* bird (*yang*). Certain trees, such as the cedar and pine, are associated with masculine strength, investing them with *yang* energy, while the flowering plum tree's delicate blossoms are balanced by the gnarled bark of the tree trunk, resulting in a harmonious balance.

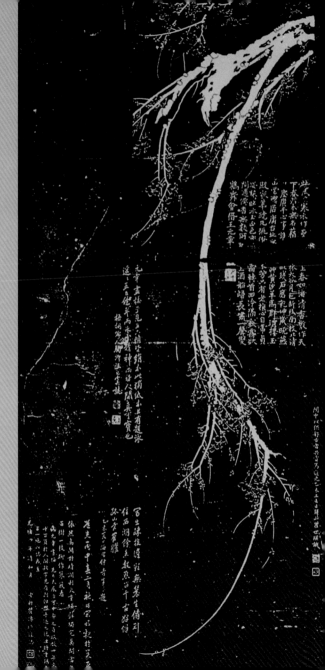

Plant and fruit symbolism in Taoist art is complex and varied; much of it refers to sexual vitality, as in both these illustrations: peaches painted on a porcelain bowl (*opposite*), China, 18th century; stone rubbing of plum blossoms in winter (*right*), China, 14th century.

Left Cloud fungus is associated with an immortal in this stone carving, China, Ming Dynasty, 17th century.

Opposite A porcelain vase, a *yin* symbol, decorated with spirit fungus, symbol of a long life and of the benefits of sexual intercourse, China, 20th century.

Fungus

the seemingly unpredictable, soft character of fungus makes it a powerful expression of the *yin* essence. So important is it in the Taoist worldview that the traditional hat – 'the fragrant cap' – worn by the true adept takes its main form from fungoid growth; it will then be decorated with objects of *yang* significance. One image of the goddess Lan Tsai-ho, surrounded by clouds (*yin*), shows her accompanied by a stag (*yang*) whose masculinity is mitigated by his bearing *yin* fungus in his mouth. Mushrooms which share the concave, swirling forms of fungi symbolize *yin* essences, but cone-shaped mushrooms – suggesting the phallus – are regarded as potently *yang*.

Dragon and phoenix

There is a satisfying serenity in the *yin/yang* polarity, the effect of balance throughout all observable worlds, both natural and mythical. *Yang* is symbolized by beasts, which appear aggressive and male, notably the stallion, the ram, the cock and, most especially, the dragon, emblem of the emperor. It is also a powerful symbol of sexual intercourse, appearing in representations of the 'leaping white tiger' or 'attack from the rear' positions. Other symbolic beasts are the reindeer, rhinoceros, *feng* bird and phoenix. The latter often represented the empress when paired with the dragon, and the two are often depicted together in Taoist temples.

Opposite left Dragon and tiger, symbols of heaven and earth, from a woodcut, Japan, 18th century.

Opposite right A dragonfish glazed ceramic finial from the roof of a Taoist temple, China, Ch'ing Dynasty, 19th century.

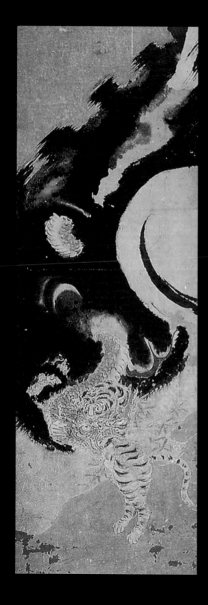

Opposite The flight of the phoenix: a silk panel showing the bird among flowers and foliage, China, Sung Dynasty, 10th–12th century.

Below A stylized bird appears on a lacquer bowl, China, Han Dynasty, 1st century BC.

INNER REFLECTIONS ON AN OUTER WORLD

It is possible, within the limitations of Western thought and language, to describe the Tao and Taoism and to identify its dominant symbols, though not very satisfactorily. Yet, there exists another vital, practical dimension: how can the Taoist best complete the equation between his or her inner self and the outer world? How can one best understand and harmonize the symbols set before and within him or her to achieve the ideals of spiritual and sexual harmony?

A Ming Dynasty porcelain dish showing Taoist children at play, symbolizing the rebirth of adepts through the practice of inner alchemy, China, Ming Dynasty, 16th–17th century.

The ideal Taoist

The ideals of Taoism are enshrined in the way of living of the immortals, the *hsien*, moving effortlessly in time and space, passing from earth to the heavens, utterly at one with the rhythms of the universe. As personifications of the finest aims of Taoism, such figures are the stuff of legend and myth, defined by the dominant symbols of the cosmos in perfect balance. Followers of Tao must be concerned with the cultivation of self and – although this may take place at the humblest level – learn to read the symbolism of the world around them as it is expressed in the polarization and, at the same time, the harmonies of *yin* and *yang*.

A Taoist priest announces to the gods of the universe that a ritual is about to begin and invites them to take part. In his hat he wears a 'flame', symbol of his inner energies now exteriorized in his communication with the heavens.

Wu wei

Opposite Harmony in the world: a soapstone seal depicts a scene from the 'Red Cliff' poem by Su Tung-p'o, China, Ming Dynasty, 16th–17th century.

Below The sense of peace evoked by the floating boat is repeated in this painting of the *Hermit Fishing*, in which the sage has clearly chosen the way of tranquillity and non-action, China, 13th century.

The principle of *wu wei* or 'non-action' is fundamental to Taoism. Attempts to interfere with the nature of things are bound to fail in the long term. But *wu wei* is not complete inaction, it is more a way of practising sympathy with natural law, of putting oneself in tune with the basic rhythms of the universe. The principle is well illustrated by the story of the pine and the willow: after a heavy snowfall the more rigid branches of the pine break under the weight of the snow, but the more supple willow branches bend, thus allowing the snow to fall to the ground.

The *Tao Te Ching* advocates, 'Do that which consists
in taking no action, and order will prevail.'

Left Quiet deliberation: a silk painting of the Eighteen Scholars, China, Song Dynasty, 10th–13th century.

Opposite Sages at a poetry contest at the orchid pavilion, Ming Dynasty; wine goblets drift on the stream, supported by leaves.

Te

Lao Tzu divided the *Tao Te Ching* into two parts: the *Tao*, or 'the way', and the *Te*, 'virtue'. But this does not mean virtue in the Western sense of moral and ethical correctness; it is rather the innate virtue of the world – its essential properties. The Taoist adept will strive for understanding of these and this will inform his or her whole life and being. True *te* is the uncontrived, unforced naturalness with which a wise person will handle practical affairs, putting his or her own wishes and desires in line with the natural flow of outside events and phenomena.

Ch'i

The fusing of the individual life with the great cosmic spirit, *ch'i*, is the object of the meditational awakening exercises practised by the Taoist adept. This spirit informs the whole of nature, animate and inanimate alike, and is the subject of an elaborate system of symbols uniting the human body with its larger, cosmic context. The head corresponds to the heavens and the hair to the stars, the eyes to the sun and the ears to the moon. Blood, coursing through the veins, is a clear symbol for the rain, feeding the streams and rivers of the landscape, which is further symbolized by the bones (mountains) and orifices (valleys). By careful observation of nature, man's destiny may be properly understood.

Opposite An earnest practitioner of *tai ch'i*, photographed in Shanghai, intent on aligning herself with the vital *ch'i* forces, expressed in the inset diagram, China, Song Dynasty, 10th–13th century.

The three crucibles

althought the Taoist avoids set patterns of behaviour and does not subscribe to a cut-and-dried code of religious practice, certain disciplines – the *neidan* or inner alchemy – are recommended to aid the understanding of self in relation to the great cosmic force. Transformation of thought through meditation eventually brings the adept into alignment with the essential currents of the universe. This awakening takes place in three crucibles within the body, the *tan t'ien*, which serve as the body's centre of gravity and meditative practice. The lowest is inside the belly, the middle one behind the solar plexus and the third, where the purified essence of the adept's thought mingles with the cosmic energies, in the head, symbol of mountains and contact with the heavens.

嬰兒現形圖

他日雲飛方見真人朝上帝

潑然直到紫微宮
一朝跳出珠光外
盟現神通不可窮
蒙籠今已化飛龍

長養聖胎
內外無塵
沈灌根株
神水溶液

小俱得其真
其神隨物化
精兆其氣枻
傳其情交葉
孕蜈蚣之子
夫蝶蛸之蟲

他云是你主人翁
我問空中誰氏子
歲包於簌簌包宇
氣穴法名無盡藏

念茲在茲
綿綿若存
抱雌守雄
衍任坐臥

此時丹熟更須慈母惜嬰兒

The Taoist yogi in meditation (*above*); his efforts to refine
his spiritual energies are symbolized by the talisman
(*opposite*), which is based on the gourd form of a crucible.

Sexual harmonies

The act of love provides Taoism with a complex and extensive body of symbols, since it so perfectly exemplifies the principles of *yin* and *yang*. Movement and position during lovemaking are themselves described in highly charged symbolic language: 'wings over the edge of the cliff'; 'cat and mouse in the hole'; 'monkey hanging from pine tree'; 'reversed flying ducks'. *Yin* and *yang* imagery provides a natural code of description for the form of the sexual organs. The male, *yang*, may be 'red bird', 'dragon pillar', or 'coral stem'. The female evokes softness and openness: 'peach', 'peony', 'golden lotus' and the 'vase which receives'. For the Taoist, the achievement of harmony in sexual relations is a vital key to a long and fruitful life.

Opposite Fusion of *yin* and *yang*: *In the Garden on a Rocky Seat*, ink and colours on silk, China, Ch'ing Dynasty, 17th–18th century.

The full life...

The *te* is also 'living well', without stress and with the full enjoyment of one's mental and physical faculties. Patience and respect must be applied to the treatment of the body, but not necessarily through following the rules of conventional medicine or dietary control. The true Taoist will learn carefully from individual experience and from sympathetic observation of the world around. Taoist literature is full of allusions to the behaviour patterns of the natural world – mammals, insects, reptiles, plants and the properties of wind and water. The superior man does not have to be an ascetic: he will take pleasure in all experiences of the physical world around him and the satisfaction of his senses, though he will be prudent and avoid self-indulgence. Indeed, he will look after himself very carefully, eating and drinking to his satisfaction, especially when preparing himself for ordeals to follow.

The good life: two *blanc-de-chine* figures of mirth and harmony, China, Ming Dynasty, 17th century.

The sage provides for the belly, not for the senses.

Lao Tzu

For the Taoist, aesthetic pleasure and harmony with nature are spiritually one, ink and colours on silk, China, Song Dynasty, 13th century.

...and a healthy one

health is a matter of great concern to
the Taoist adept and, like sex, medicine
provides a rich vocabulary of symbols.
Indeed, perhaps the central symbol for
the truly wise man, the Taoist sage, is the
doctor, with his knowledge of the inner
ebb and flow of the bodily forces and their
relationship with those of the world
outside. In more physical terms, the body
is seen as a field of currents, based on
the central circulation pattern, hence,
the importance in traditional Chinese
medicine of acupuncture, which seeks
to regulate the flow of *ch'i* throughout
the body. Mental energies are likewise
to be stimulated and cared for; the act
of consulting the *I Ching*, for instance,
is in itself beneficial.

Care for man's inner
force centres (*below*)
ensures a continued
thriving market in
traditional herbal
medicines, on sale here
on a holy mountain at
Emei, Sichuan, China
(*opposite*).

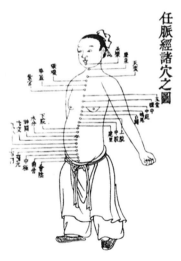

The Tao 473

In a home it is the site that matters.

Lao Tzu

The lie of the land

The vital streams of energy, which enliven the body and the mind, have their counterpart in the veins and streams of the natural world. Chinese landscape painting is characterized by the emphasis given to the 'dragon veins', which run in all directions; the artist will skilfully relate them to form an overall pattern to reveal the true lie of the land. Before a house is built many people in China will call in the services of a geomancer, the *feng shui* man, literally the 'wind and water' man, who will work out the direction and location of the structure in relation to the vital energy currents in the land. Such subtle relationships are also found in the traditional Zen hard gardens, in which the rocks, representing mountains, seem to float in a 'sea' of immaculately raked gravel.

The *feng shui* man might express the forces of the land in such a diagram as this (*opposite right*) while the serious artist will seek to express the 'dragon veins', the flow of power through the landscape, in a harmonious composition (*opposite left*), *Flowering Hills in the Height of Spring* by Lan Ying, China, Ming Dynasty, 17th century.

The tranquil Taoist

according to the book of *Chuang Tzu*, an old man is seen by some followers of Confucius swimming in a raging torrent; suddenly, he disappears. The pupils of Confucius rush to save him, but the man reaches the bank entirely unaided. Asked how he had pulled off this remarkable feat of survival, the man replied that he had simply let himself go with the descending and ascending currents in the water. The true Taoist, in other words, moulds his or her senses, body and mind until they are at one with the currents of the world without.

Opposite Shen Chou (1427–1509) wrote a poem to accompany his ink and colour painting *Reading in the Autumn* which ends 'My spirit has gone wandering in the sky… Who can fathom it?'

Overleaf All is harmony among the *hsien* in the Taoist heaven, embroidered silk panel, China, 18th century.

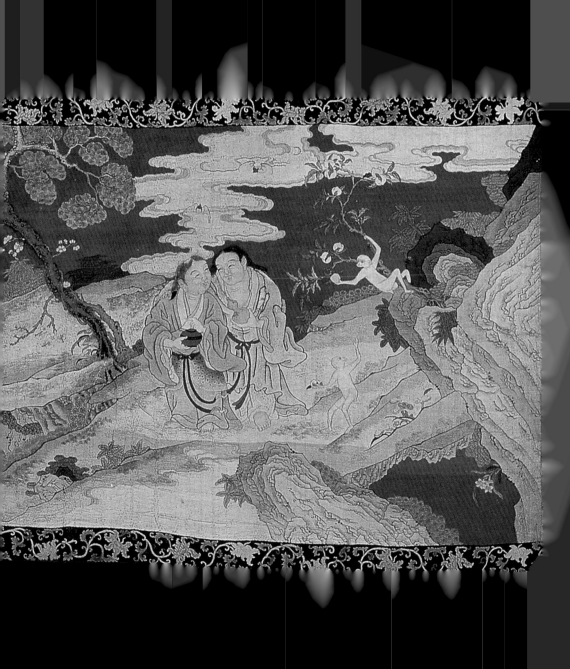

Christianity

SYMBOL AND SACRAMENT

Over the centuries Christians have regarded physical phenomena as symbolizing and revealing spiritual truths. Jesus himself inspired this way of looking at the world: at the beginning of his ministry he was baptised in the river Jordan, the puryifying water symbolizing spiritual cleansing. As Jesus broke bread at the Last Supper, just before his crucifixion, he said that it represented his body; as he poured out wine, he declared it represented his blood.

Fearful of persecution, the early Christians used symbolism to conceal their worship of Jesus as the son of God. Jesus was often depicted as a fish, since the letters of the Greek word for fish (*ichthus*) were

Page 480 Coloured enamel panel set in jewelled frame showing Christ as ruler or judge, St Mark's Basilica, Venice, 13th century.

Opposite A Spanish carved gravestone with the image of a fish – a symbol of Christ – over a bowl, 13th century.

seen as an acrostic for the first letters of 'Jesus Christ, Son of God, the Saviour'. Christian saints were likewise identified symbolically in the early church. The Revelation of St John the Divine refers enigmatically to a lion, a calf, a beast with the face of a man and a flying eagle worshipping before God's throne. Fourth-century Christians saw these as representing the four Evangelists, respectively: St Mark, who begins his Gospel in the wilderness, the haunt of lions; St Luke, who starts with

Above Early Christian stone with images of concealed worship, including a cross disguised as an anchor and the Greek word for fish, *ichthus*.

Opposite Christ in glory framed by symbolic representations of the four Evangelists, a page from the illuminated Westminster Psalter, England, *c.* 1250.

a sacrifice, hence the ox calf; St Matthew, who records the human ancestors of Jesus; and St John, whose lofty theology shares the sky with the eagle.

The very sacraments of Christianity are effectively outward and visible signs of inward and spiritual grace. Two were instituted by Jesus (baptism and the Holy Communion) and many Christians recognize five others: confirmation, penance, holy orders, annointing of the sick and marriage.

The triptych altarpiece of the *Seven Sacraments* by Rogier van der Weyden, *c.* 1445–50, illustrates the sacraments of Christianity.

In the early 14th-century painting *Christ on the Tree of Life* by Pacino da Bonaguido, divine history is symbolically divided into twelve segments.

THE CHRISTIAN YEAR

Scarcely any date in the traditional Christian year is directly specified in the Bible. Only the date of Jesus' crucifixion has scriptural warranty, since it coincided with the Jewish springtime Passover celebration. Yet to divide the year into a series of Christian festivals makes symbolic sense, to enable believers to rejoice in and worship aspects of the Christian faith. Once the date of Christ's birth was assigned, his conception was simple to calculate. Over time other annual feasts were added to the Christian year, including the feasts of All Saints and All Souls, as well as the season of Lent, commemorating the forty days which Jesus spent fasting in the wilderness. On 15 August, Catholics celebrate the Assumption into Heaven of the Virgin Mary, mother of Jesus.

Lady Day

according to the Gospel of St Luke, the Angel Gabriel appeared on God's behalf to a young virgin named Mary in the Galilean town of Nazareth and told her that God was with her and she was highly favoured. He then announced, 'You shall conceive and bear a son, and you shall give him the name Jesus' (Luke 1:31).

In depicting the scene of the Annunciation, artists frequently include a white lily, symbol of Mary's purity, while the Virgin usually wears a gown of lapis lazuli blue, reflecting her role as Queen of Heaven. The Christian church celebrates the Annunciation on 25 March, which is known as Lady Day.

Opposite The opening page of a Book of Hours showing the Annunciation, attributed to Zebo da Firenze, *c.* 1405–10.

Below Woodcut of a lily, symbol of the Virgin Mary, from the 1485 German publication *Hortus Sanitatis.*

omnie labia me
a apnes
tos meum
annunciabu laudem tuam.

Christmas

nothing in the Bible indicates the day on which Jesus was born, but three centuries or so after his birth Christians began to associate the date with the winter solstice, the day on which the sun is reborn. Hence the feast of the Nativity began to be celebrated on 25 December.

The biblical story records that Mary and her husband Joseph had arrived at Bethlehem when she was about to give birth and, according to St Luke's gospel, they could find no room in any inn and had to stay in a stable, and there Jesus was born.

Finding no room in the inn, Jesus is identified with the world's outcasts, while his birth in Bethlehem, the city of King David, associates the Christian messiah with Israel's greatest king.

Once in royal
  David's city
Stood a lowly
  cattle shed,
Where a mother
  laid her baby
In a manger for
  his bed:
Mary was that
  mother mild,
Jesus Christ her
  little child.

Cecil Frances Alexander, 'Once in royal David's city', 1848.

Epiphany

a tradition originating in the Eastern Orthodox Churches fixes 6 January as the date when three wise men, the Magi, guided by a heavenly star, came to worship the infant Jesus. 'Entering the house, they saw the child with Mary his mother, and bowed to the ground in homage to him; then they opened their treasures and offered him gifts, gold, frankincense and myrrh' (Matthew 2:11). The three gifts can be understood symbolically: gold for kingship, frankincense for divinity, and myrrh (used in embalming) to represent Jesus' death.

Above The symbol of Christ appears between angels in a detail from the carved ivory cover of the *Lorsch Gospels*, Germany, early 9th century.

Opposite The Adoration of the Kings by Jan Gossaert, 1510–15, shows the three Magi.

**What can I give him,
Poor as I am?
If I were a shepherd
I would bring a lamb,
If I were a wise man
I would do my part
Yet what I can I give him,
Give my heart.**

Christina Rossetti, 'In the bleak midwinter', 1872.

The Temptation of Christ, Duccio, 1308–11, shows Christ rejecting
the devil's enticements.

Lent

derived from the Old English word for spring
(*lencten*), Lent comprises the forty days leading
up to Easter (excluding Sundays), beginning on
Ash Wednesday. It commemorates the forty days
that Jesus spent fasting in the wilderness, and as
a result is a time for abstinence for many
Christian believers.

During his time in the wilderness, Jesus resisted
ongoing temptation by Satan to misuse his divine
powers. These temptations were: first to turn
stones into bread; second to worship the devil,
who in return promised to give him authority
over all the kingdoms of the world; and third, to
leap from a tower of the Temple, knowing that
God would save him. Jesus, with the power of
the Holy Spirit, was able to resist all of the
temptations, and returned to his disciples.

A woodcut of the devil, from the *Compendium maleficarum,* a
treatise on witchcraft, published in 1626.

Detail of the
Resurrection from
the *Isenheim
Altarpiece*, Matthias
Grünewald,
1512–16.

Easter

On Good Friday Jesus was crucified, outside the walls of Jerusalem for claiming to be the king of the Jews. Three days later women came to his tomb to anoint his body, only to find the tomb empty. Jesus then appeared and spoke to his follower Mary Magdalene, who did not at first recognize him: 'Jesus said to her "Why are you weeping? Who is it you are looking for?" Thinking it was the gardener, she said, if it is you, sir, who removed him, tell me where you have laid him, and I will take him away' (John 20:15).

As the gardener, Jesus is seen to recreate the garden of Eden from which humanity had been expelled. He forbids Mary from touching him, but charges her with spreading the news to his followers of his resurrection. Easter is celebrated on a Sunday to mark Christ's rising from the dead on the third day.

Woodcut of *Noli me tangere (Small Passion)*, Albrecht Dürer, 1509–11. Mary Magdalene mistakes the risen Christ for a gardener, as she weeps by the empty tomb.

Ascension

For forty days after his resurrection Jesus stayed with his followers, continuing to teach them. It is believed that he was with his disciples near the Mount of Olives east of Jerusalem, when he ascended into heaven. There are various accounts of how this happened: he lifted up his hands and blessed his followers, and was

carried up into heaven; he was lifted up and a cloud received him from their sight; he was taken up into heaven and sat down at the right hand of God. Sometimes Jesus is shown with his hands outstretched in blessing during his ascension. A favourite device of many early Christian artists was to depict God's hand, appearing from the heavens, to help pull Jesus up.

See! he lifts his hands above: Alleluya!
See! he shows the prints of love: Alleluya!
Hark! his gracious lips bestow: Alleluya!
Blessings on his Church below: Alleluya!

Charles Wesley, 'Hail the day that sees him rise', 1739.

Above The Passional of Christ and Antichrist, Lucas Cranach the Elder, woodcut, 1521.

Opposite The Ascension, from a Carolingian illumination, *c.* 842.

Pentecost

Sometimes known as Whitsunday, the feast of Pentecost celebrates the gift of the Holy Spirit to the followers of Jesus and takes place fifty days after Easter. *The Acts of the Apostles* describes what happened as Jesus' twelve disciples were all together in one place: 'Suddenly there came from the sky a noise like that of a strong driving wind, which filled the whole house where they were sitting. And there appeared to them tongues like flames of fire, dispersed among them and resting on each one. And they were all filled with the Holy Spirit and began to talk in other tongues, as the Spirit gave them power of utterance' (Acts 2:2–4).

Christian art traditionally depicts the Virgin Mary at the centre of this group, and often adds to the symbol of fire that of the dove (the Old Testament symbol of peace) to represent God's Holy Spirit descending upon Jesus when he was baptized.

In the *Mysteries of the Rosary* by Vincenzo Campi, 16th century, the Holy Spirit is represented as a dove above the group of apostles.

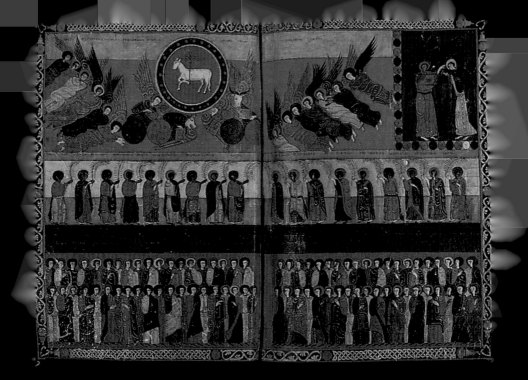

The *Adoration of the Mystic Lamb*, illuminated manuscript of Beatus' *Commentary on the Apocalypse*, c. 1047.

For all the saints who from their labours rest,
Who thee by faith before the world confest,
Thy name, O Jesu, be for ever blest. Alleluya!
Thou wast their Rock, their Fortress and their Might;
Thou, Lord, their Captain in the well-fought fight,
Thou in the darkness drear their one true Light. Alleluya

All Saints

Celebrated in Western Christendom on 1 November (and by Eastern Orthodox Christians on the first Sunday after Pentecost), this feast commemorates all the saints and martyrs of the Christian church. Instituted as a day of obligation in 835, it is known in Old English as All Hallows, hence the name Halloween for the previous day, which in past times was often celebrated with merriment and bonfires. In works of art, the saints and martyrs are usually shown lined up worshipping Jesus, represented as the Lamb of God.

Palm leaf and olive branch, symbols of triumph and peace, respectively, from an embossing in the early Christian catacombs.

All Souls

On 2 November 998, Odilo, abbot of the monastery of Cluny in France, instructed his monks to make special prayers on behalf of the dead. The practice spread through Western Christendom, and 2 November became known as All Souls' Day. Christian iconography, in sculpture and painting, often depicts the souls of the righteous being carried to heaven by angels. An exquisite late 12th-century or early 13th-century sculpture in the abbey of St Denis, Paris, portrays righteous souls safe in the bosom of Abraham: 'But the souls of the just are in God's hand, and torment shall not touch them' (Wisdom 3:1–2).

Here they live in endless life;
Transience has passed away;
Here they bloom, here thrive, they flourish,
For decayed is all decay.

St Peter Damien, 1007–72

Above Detail from St Michael raising souls, *The Shaftesbury Psalter*, England, mid 12th century.

Opposite Commendation of the souls, *Hasting Hours*, Flanders, 1475–83.

A giant carved runestone, one of two such stones, located in present-day Jelling, Denmark. The stone, erected by King Harald Bluetooth (*c.* 980) commemorates the Danish conversion to Christianity.

CROSS AND CRUCIFIX

Crucifixion was the most humiliating death the Romans could impose. Roman citizens condemned to death (such as St Paul) would assert their right to die by the sword, not on a cross. Yet the cross became the most potent symbol of the glory of Christianity. Christians took up the notion that Jesus willingly submitted to crucifixion rather than call upon God, his Heavenly Father, to bring divine retribution on those who were tormenting him. He forgave those who crucified him with the words, 'Father, forgive them; they do not know what they are doing' (Luke 23:34).

Gravestone with a Celtic cross, 9th–10th century.

Crucified for me, dear Jesus, fasten my whole self to you with the nails of your love.

St Bernardino of Siena, 1380–1444

The tree of life

at one point the New Testament describes Jesus as being hanged not on a cross but on a tree. This is a reference to the story in the book of Genesis of how Adam and Eve brought sin and death into the world by eating the forbidden fruit of a tree in the Garden of Eden. They were expelled from Paradise as punishment for their transgression. By submitting to crucifixion, yet forgiving those who crucified him, and by rising from the dead and bringing the hope of resurrection, Jesus was seen as reversing the condemnation of Adam and Eve. The cross on which he died thus became the tree of life.

Right Wooden plague cross, 14th century.

Opposite The Tree of Life and Death, manuscript illumination, Berthold Furtmeyer, 1481.

The tree on which were fixed his dying limbs was still the chair of the Master teaching.

St Augustine, 354–430

The lamb of God

When John the Baptist first saw Jesus he cried, 'There is the Lamb of God; it is he who takes away the sin of the world' (John 1:29–30). The lamb as a sacrificial victim is a long-standing Judeo-Christian tradition. In the Old Testament story of the flight of the Jews from Egypt, it is through marking their doors with the blood of a sacrificial lamb that the Jews are saved from death and eventually led into the promised land. Many Christians see this as a foretelling of the sacrifice of Jesus Christ who, through the shedding of his innocent blood, atones for the sins of humankind and guarantees eternal salvation for all.

Artists often depict Jesus as the *Agnus Dei* (Lamb of God) who carries or stands by a cross, or sometimes a banner painted with a red cross.

Above Sandstone relief of John the Baptist baptizing two noblemen, 1040.

Opposite Detail of the lamb from an illuminated manuscript of Beatus *Commentary on the Apocalypse, c.* 1047.

The tortured Christ

Below A medieval relief of Christ being nailed to the cross, the Cathedral of St Marien, Havelberg, Germany.

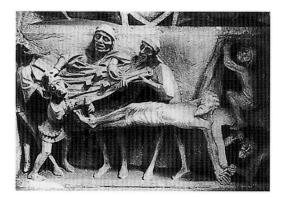

One interpretation of Jesus' crucifixion is to see it as representing his solidarity with all those who suffer or are unjustly tortured. In the early 16th century Matthias Grünewald painted a superb representation of this for the Antonites of Isenheim in Alsace, monastic followers of the early Christian St Anthony of Egypt. Grünewald depicted the crucified Jesus as pock-marked and rotting, his blood-spattered body green and decaying. The Antonites ran a hospital to nurse sufferers from disease and Grünewald's dying Jesus is symbolically identified with them.

Opposite The Crucifixion from the *Isenheim Altarpiece*, Matthias Grünewald, 1512–16.

**His dying crimson like a robe
Spreads o'er his body on the tree;
Then I am dead to all the globe,
And all the globe is dead to me.**

Isaac Watts, 'When I survey the
wondrous cross', 1707

The glory of the cross

St Paul wrote that the crucifixion seems folly to those who are perishing, but to those who are being saved it is the power of God. The cross was no tragedy 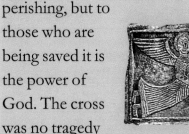 or error on the part of Jesus but a death deliberately chosen by him in obedience to his Heavenly Father. Christian art often symbolizes this divine scheme by depicting the crucified Jesus as supported by God the Father, while the Holy Spirit – in the form of a dove – descends on the crucified's head. Because of this, Jesus is sometimes portrayed on the cross as splendidly crowned and robed.

He gave power unto the sharp thorns to enter and most cruelly wound his divine and trembling head; he himself gave power to the hard nails to enter his tender feet and hands.

Angela of Foligno, *The Book of Divine Consolation, c.* 1248–1309

Above Relief depicting Christ between two angels, church of Santa Maria de Quintanilla de las Viñas, Spain, 7th century.

Opposite The Holy Trinity, 15th-century Austrian painting.

Instruments of the Passion

'Passion', deriving from the Latin word for suffering, refers to the last week of Jesus' earthly life, above all to his trial, torture and crucifixion. Nails pierced his hands and feet as he was fixed to the cross. A crown of thorns was forced on to his head. A whip recalls his scourging. When he cried, 'I thirst,' a sponge with vinegar was applied to his lips. Alongside the hammer, which drove in the nails, a pair of pincers appears, which pulled out the nails at his deposition. Sometimes artists depicting these instruments of the Passion include the ladder down which his dead body was dragged.

Above Mexican stone cross carved with the face of Christ, the crown of thorns and the instruments of the Passion, 17th century.

Opposite Detail from *The Agony in the Garden*, Andrea Mantegna, *c.* 1460.

Stigmata

On the cross, Jesus was wounded five times. Nails pierced his hands and feet. To make sure that he was dead, a Roman soldier plunged a spear into his side. From the Greek word *stigma* (mark), these wounds came to be called Jesus' stigmata. Throughout Christian history men and women intensely meditating on the crucifixion have found such marks on their own bodies. The first person to bear these stigmata was St Francis of Assisi, the purple wounds appearing on his body as he prayed at La Verna, Italy in 1224.

Left Biblical crown of thorns, from an Old English engraving.

Opposite The Stigmatization of Saint Francis, painted wooden panel, Sassetta, *c.* 1437–44.

The keys of St Peter

J esus asked his disciples, ' "Who do you say I am?" Peter answered: "You are the Messiah, the Son of the living God." ' In response Jesus said: ' "I will give you the keys of the kingdom of Heaven; what you forbid on earth shall be forbidden in heaven, and what you allow on earth shall be allowed in heaven" ' (Matthew 16:16–17, 19).

St Peter's symbol is thus a pair of keys. But he also once betrayed Jesus, claiming when Jesus was on trial never to have known him. When Peter reached Rome, he too was martyred, but (legend has it) insisted that he should be crucified upside down, so as to be lower than his Lord. Therefore, a second symbol of this disciple is a cross turned upside-down.

Opposite The crucifixion of St Peter, detail of the *Stefaneschi Triptych*, Giotto, *c.* 1320.

Below Stone statue of St Peter with the keys of the Kingdom of Heaven, 12th century.

The cross of St Andrew

a fisherman, St Andrew was recruited, with his brother Peter, to be the first disciples of Jesus. A 4th-century tradition tells that he was crucified, but remained alive for two days, preaching the Gospel from the cross. A later tradition declares that the cross was X-shaped (the saltire cross), representing the first letter of the Greek word for Christ. Andrew is the patron saint of Greece, Romania, Russia and Scotland, whose national flag is a saltire cross.

Jesus said, 'Come with me, and I will make you fishers of men.'

Matthew 4:19

QUEEN OF HEAVEN

Madonna is Italian for 'my lady' and signifies the mother of Jesus, the Blessed Virgin Mary, particularly when in art she is depicted carrying her son Jesus, either in her womb or on her knee. The New Testament asserts that she conceived Jesus without losing her virginity. And since she was the mother of one who brought grace and forgiveness to the world, eventually many Christians have looked to her as their greatest protectress among all the saints. In spite of her exalted state, Mary is also a symbol of Christian humility. Nevertheless her depiction often reflects her glory, as she is seen with a halo of stars and on a crescent moon.

Opposite This detail of *The Immaculate Conception* by Diego Velázquez *c.* 1618, depicts the Virgin Mary standing on the moon, crowned by a halo of stars.

'Ave Maria'

according to the Gospel of St Luke, Elizabeth, the mother of St John the Baptist, declared to her cousin Mary, the mother of Jesus, 'God's blessing it on you above all women, and his blessing is on the fruit of your womb' (Luke 1:42). Since the Middle Ages, this has been one of Christendom's most celebrated prayers: 'Ave Maria, gratia plena, Dominus tecum. Benedicta tu in mulieribus, et benedictus fructus ventris tui, Jesus.' To this many add the request, 'Holy Mary, Mother of God, pray for us sinners, now and at the hour of our death.' Many Christians use this prayer in connection with the rosary, a string of prayer beads used as a devotional device. While praying the beads of the rosary, the faithful repeatedly pray, 'Ave Maria'.

Opposite Madonna of the Rosary, Caravaggio, 1606–7.

Christic child

Images of the infant Jesus have offered scope for rich symbolism. Usually he is guarded by his mother, who may well be crowned Queen of Heaven and carry a sceptre as well as her divine son. The child is often portrayed seated upright, blessing the world. Other artists include the Virgin Mary's mother, St Anne. Leonardo da Vinci's *The Virgin of the Rocks* draws on another rich symbolic tradition. Here Jesus' mother is blessing her son with one hand, while with her other hand she caresses the infant John the Baptist (identified by one of his symbols, a cross with a long stem), whose mother was Mary's cousin. In Leonardo's painting John is kneeling in prayer, while Jesus blesses him. An angel behind the Christ child holds the chubby divine baby upright.

Opposite The Virgin of the Rocks, Leonardo da Vinci, *c.* 1491–1508.

Pietà

Opposite The *Lamentation over the Dead Christ*, Rembrandt, *c.* 1635.

Below The marble *Pietà* by Michelangelo in St Peter's Basilica, Vatican City, *c.* 1500.

Pietà, Italian for 'pity', in art refers to depictions of the Blessed Virgin Mary holding the body of her dead son across her knees. Among the most exquisite is Michelangelo's sculpture in St Peter's Basilica, Rome; among the most sombre, is one by Rembrandt. Michelangelo's *Pietà* was criticized because he made the mother of Jesus seem younger than her son. His reply was that because of her purity she possessed eternal youth. He also clad her in brilliantly sculpted clothing, which in the words of the famous art critic John Ruskin, represented the spirit of repose, 'repose saintly and severe'. Ruskin added that the undulation of the clothing follows the dances of angels.

The Assumption

Below The Assumption of the Virgin, detail from the west portal of Senlis Cathedral, France, *c.* 1170.

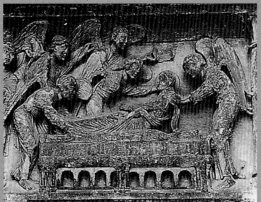

although the notion that after her death the Blessed Virgin Mary was taken up body and soul into heaven was declared an official belief of Roman Catholics only in 1950, her Assumption has long been relished as a subject of Christian art. In the 15th and 16th centuries a galaxy of artists depicted the scene, in particular Gerolamo da Vicenza, Titian and the sculptor Tilman Riemenschneider, transforming the event into one of immense spectacle.

Opposite The Dormition and Assumption of the Virgin, Gerolamo da Vicenza, 1488.

Protectress

One of the most powerful symbols of the Madonna is her role as protectress of humanity. Usually she is represented in a cloak, which she opens wide to shelter vulnerable men and women who share her humanity and desire her care. They are often depicted as the most powerful in the world – sovereigns, popes, bishops, noble lords and ladies – as well as the humble folk who also display some part of Mary's own humility.

Opposite The Virgin Mary, painted central panel, *Polyptych of the Misericordia*, Piero della Francesca, 1445–62.

Below Madonna Carrying in her Womb God the Father and his Crucified Son, painted wood, 15th century.

Yet, to shame the wise, God has chosen what the world counts folly, and to shame what is strong, God has chosen what the world counts weakness.

I Corinthians 1:27–28

Black Madonna, painted wood, Church of Santa Maria Liberatrice, Ancona, 16th century.

Black Madonna

In Europe alone, there are hundreds of depictions of the Virgin Mary as a Black Madonna, and many have become the focus of pilgrimage, such as those at Rocamadour in France and Czestochowa in Poland. Yet there is no definitive explanation for why so many dark-coloured images exist. Some believe that the colour was original, deriving from a combination of Christian imagery and pagan goddess worship, while others believe the colours have deepened over time due to candle soot in churches and chemical changes in the paint. Some Christians claim a Judeo-Christian precedent in the Jewish scriptures of the Old Testament, in which a dark woman reciting a love poem sings, 'I am dark but lovely' (Song of Songs 1:5).

LEGEND

Though often historically dubious, legends can evoke potent echoes in the human psyche. The Christian tradition is replete with them, many surrounded with expressive symbols. Many places in Christendom claim to have inherited the chalice from which Jesus and his disciples drank at their last meal on earth, without any real grounds for their claims. Other believers wondered what had happened to the shroud in which Jesus was wrapped at his burial. Such legendary symbols have been matched in the Christian tradition by remarkable images, often derived from the imagination of the Christian fathers.

Opposite Souls Cross over the Narrow Bridge, fresco in the church of Santa Maria in Piano, Loreto Aprutino, Italy, 13th century.

The kind of religion
which is without stain
or fault in the sight of
God our Father is this:
to go to the help of
orphans and widows in
their distress and keep
oneself untarnished by
the world.

James 1:27

The pilgrim

St James the Great is the patron saint of pilgrims.
Although he was executed and buried in the Holy Land,
his body is said to rest today at Santiago de Compostela
in Spain, which (after Jerusalem and Rome) is the most
important pilgrimage centre in Christendom. Christian
art depicts him covered in symbols: a scallop shell, from
the shores of Galicia; a pilgrim's staff; a hat, since
pilgrims travel through inhospitable lands during the
heat of the day; and a flask for water. And whereas most
saints are depicted barefoot, St James, because of his
long journeys, often wears boots.

Opposite left A 12th-century sculpture of St James of Compostela
carrying a staff and a purse decorated with a scallop shell.

Opposite right A cross from the bishop's throne at Torcello
Cathedral, Italy, early medieval period.

Holy Blood, Holy Grail

The legend of the Holy Grail records that the chalice which Jesus used at his Last Supper with his disciples was retrieved by a devout Jew, Joseph of Arimathea, who also provided a tomb for Jesus. As Jesus was dying on the cross, Joseph, it is said, used this chalice to catch some of his spilled blood. The story

becomes yet more fanciful. Joseph, it was claimed, next visited England. Arriving at Glastonbury, he left the Grail there, where it was buried and long forgotten. Certainly there is no trace at Glastonbury of such a symbol today; but many other places still claim to possess a drop of Jesus' Holy Blood.

A woodcut illustrating *The Imitation of Christ*, a 15th-century book of Christian devotion written by Thomas à Kempis.

Angels holding the Holy Grail in an illumination from the *Playfair Book of Hours*, Rouen, France, late 15th century.

The shroud of Turin

Joseph of Arimathea, says St Matthew's Gospel, took the body of the dead Jesus 'and wrapped it in a clean linen sheet' (Matthew 27:59). From 1578, in the chapel of the Dukes of Savoy close by Turin Cathedral, a length of ivory-coloured material bearing a strange image of a bearded man was exhibited as the same shroud. The image displays wounds in exactly the same places as those inflicted on Jesus at his crucifixion. Today, most scholars believe that this shroud is a fake. Its history cannot be traced back beyond the 14th century. Yet, as the French poet Paul Claudel wrote, the image on the shroud is 'so frightening and yet so beautiful that one can escape it only by worship'.

This much (and this
  is all) we know,
They are supremely blest,
Have done with sin, and
  care, and woe,
And with their Saviour rest.

John Newton, 'On the Death of a Believer', 1779

Opposite Head of Christ, detail from the Turin shroud.

The Glastonbury thorn

Opposite Joseph of Arimathea Planting his Staff at Glastonbury, illumination, Brotherhood of St Seraphim of Sarov, 1978.

When Joseph of Arimathea came to England, he bequeathed to Glastonbury not only the Holy Grail but also his staff. Joseph stuck it into the ground, where it took root and was transformed into a hawthorn. Glastonbury hawthorns are unusual in that they bloom in May and again around Christmas, but whether they are descended from the staff of Joseph of Arimathea is a moot point. The monks of Glastonbury Abbey certainly promoted the story, which brought them pilgrims and renown. In the mid 17th century the original tree was destroyed by Puritans, but it is claimed that cuttings survived.

S. JOSEPH OF ARIMATHEA

Chi-rho

the monogram *chi-rho* derives from the first two letters of the Greek word for Christ, and is represented by the symbols X and P, Greek capital letters. One 5th-century bronze cross is fascinating for incorporating these letters with two other Greek ones, 'alpha' and 'omega', the first and last letters of the Greek alphabet and another symbol of Jesus: ' "I am Alpha and Omega" says the Lord, who is, and who was, and who is to come, the sovereign Lord of all' (Revelation 1:8).

I know much Greek and Latin. I have still to learn the alphabet of how to become a saint.

St Arsenius, 354–450

Above Bronze cross with monogram *chi-rho* and the symbols 'alpha' and 'omega', 5th century.

Opposite Jewelry depicting the *chi-rho*, 4th century.

St Veronica

as Jesus made his way to be crucified, carrying his own cross, the four Gospels add these details: a man named Simon of Cyrene was forced to help carry the cross; women lamented what was happening, and Jesus paused to speak with them; he was stripped of his garments. One episode not found in the Gospels tells of a woman, later named Veronica, who wiped the sweat from his face. Jesus went on his way, and she discovered that an image of his face had been imprinted on the cloth or handkerchief she had used. Although many places in Christendom have claimed to possess this cloth, the Roman clergy insisted that theirs was the true image, *vera icon*, hence the name 'Veronica'.

Above Veronica with the Sudarium, Master of St Veronica, *c.* 1420.

Opposite Christ Making his Way to his Crucifixion, stone altarpiece, *c.* 1500.

St Michael

'Then war broke out in heaven. Michael and his angels waged war upon the dragon. The dragon and his angels fought, but they had not the strength to win, and no foothold was left them in heaven. So the great dragon was thrown down, that serpent of old that led the whole world astray, whose name is Satan, or the Devil – thrown down to the earth, and his angels with him' (Revelation 12: 7–9).

St Michael is thus often portrayed winged and sometimes riding a charger, plunging his spear or sword into a serpent. Additionally, as Michael the Archangel, he is shown holding a pair of scales, with which he weighs the souls of the dead.

Awake! Be on the alert! Your enemy the devil, like a roaring lion, prowls round looking for someone to devour.

1 Peter 5:8

Above The Archangel Michael Vanquishing the Devil, illumination, 1490.

Opposite The Archangel Michael and his Angels Defeating the Forces of Evil, illumination, 11th century.

DEVS QVI

Revelation

The last book of the Bible, the Revelation of St John the Divine, overflows with imagery and symbol, including this compelling vision of Jesus glorified: 'I saw seven standing lamps of gold, and among the lamps one like a son of man, robed down to his feet, with a golden girdle round his breast. The hair of his head was white as snow-white wool, and his eyes flamed like fire; his feet gleamed like burnished brass refined in a furnace, and his voice was like the sound of rushing waters. In his right hand he held seven stars, and out of his mouth came a sharp two-edged sword; and his face shone like the sun in full strength' (Revelation 1: 12–16).

The Four Horsemen of the Apocalypse, illumination, *Apocalypse of St Sever*, France, 11th century.

Mysteries

The Mandala

THE CIRCLE
AND THE CENTRE

Although most immediately associated with the religions of India and Tibet, the mandala, literally 'circle', is one of the most potent symbols of humankind. Its circular form and concentric structure reflect the shape of the universe outside and the sense of perfection within. Concentration on its form and content is an aid to prayer and meditation, leading eventually to a complete ability to be at one with the world.

This cosmic mandala fresco in the Temple Court of the Paro Dzong fortress, Bhutan, incorporates the 'mystic spiral', representation of the primary movement of the universe.

Page 560 An 18th-century Tibetan hanging painting of the Supreme Buddha Vajrasattva, synthesizing mandalas.

The cosmic mandala

representation of the universe as a series of concentric rings has been common in many cultures, consistently reappearing in art and ritual. In this context, the mandala can be seen as an evocation of the universe, of galaxies swirling around a centre, of planets revolving around the sun. At the same time, it is a model of the soul's journey from the periphery to the centre of all understanding. This is a journey common to the initiates of Tantric practices, the aborigines of Australasia and even psychiatric patients in search of wholeness in a fragmented world.

Representations of the universe and its orbits, surrounded by outer space, may be used as meditational aids, their circular form suggesting a simple mandala, as in this 17th-century example from Gujarat, India.

The island continent

althougth the cosmograms of Tantric belief were
certainly a way of codifying external phenomena and of
organizing current knowledge of the universe, their
mandala-like forms lent them a complexity of functions.
They are focused on a single point, the mythical Mount
Meru, around which is the earth, Jambudvipa, with
concentric circles representing cosmic fields, spheres
and atmospheric zones within the sphere, which
separates the visible from the non-visible world. In
Tantric belief the central point of Mount Meru may also
be identified with the centre point of the human body –
thus a person becomes at one with the universe, which
radiates as a flat circle outward from the spinal column,
the *merudanda*, or 'rod of Meru'.

Opposite Meditation on formal representations of the universe is designed
to achieve identification with the fundamental forces of the cosmos.
Cosmographical diagrams, such as this 18th-century painted cloth
from Rajasthan, India, show Jambudvipa, the island continent,
surrounded by energy fields and atmospheric zones.

Movement and rest

the image of the cosmos as a still point around which various degrees of creation turn is applicable in many contexts. It may be made immensely complex by having the centre occupied by a potent religious image: the Buddha, perhaps, or a temple, with other saints and icons at the cardinal points. In its simplest yet most intense form, the centre of the Hindu and Buddhist mandala is the *derata*, the ultimate divine principle, uniting object and subject as they spin out from the centre, which may be cosmic, but which may equally be that of the human body.

Opposite This 17th-century gouache mandala from Rajasthan, India is a simple yet potent symbol of the cosmos in simultaneous evolution and dissolution, in tension and repose. In yoga, this symbol is the powerful enneagram, whose exact meaning must remain a secret but which is universally known to invoke perpetual motion and perpetual rest simultaneously.

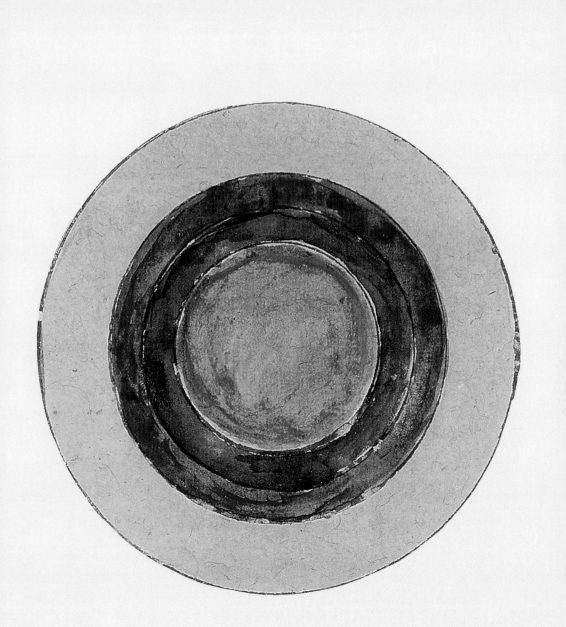

The Mandala 569

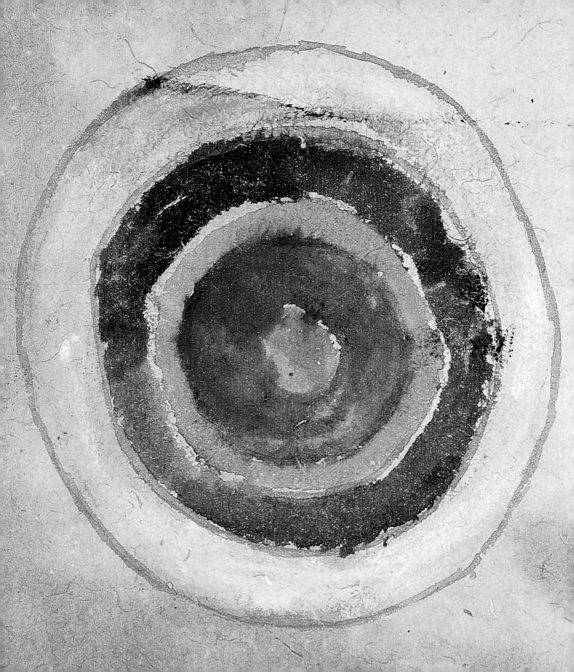

A map of the cosmos

So the mandala is no longer a cosmogram but a psycho-cosmogram, the scheme of the disintegration from the one to the many and of reintegration from the many to the one, to that absolute consciousness, entire and luminous.

Giuseppe Tucci, *The Theory and Practice of the Mandala*

Opposite The essential, universal pattern of the mandala is beautifully expressed in this simple 17th-century gouache from Uttar Pradesh, India. Its representation of the limitless space of the cosmos also symbolizes all essential structures – the society which rotates around the throne of the king, the universe around its central mountain and the movement of our own bodies around an internal axial point.

the mandala is both a universal symbol and a symbol of the universe. But its use in the rituals and liturgies of various religions and, indeed, in modern psychoanalysis is only a part of its whole significance; it is also the essential plan of the whole universe, balancing centrifugal and centripetal forces, combining beginning and end. It is the ultimate symbol of wholeness; its centre is unity, equidistant from every point of the outer curve of the circle. In grasping the whole significance of this symbol, the individual – whatever his or her culture – experiences a sense of liberation, which comes from the realization of the unity of all phenomena and experience.

A gateway to the divine

The potency of concentric circles around a centre point, the most intense expression of the divine, pervades many cultures and religions. Among the Huichol tribes of California and Mexico, such a vision of circles, the *nierika*, is a prayer offering, a reflection of the face of the god and a means of realizing the most concentrated experience of the sacred, symbolized by the centre point.

This contemporary painting by Michael Brown (Rising Eagle) shows a celebrant and a symbolic slain deer before a great *nierika*.

A Chinese mirror

Certain early Chinese mirrors are effectively mandalas, classic schemes of the universe: the circles of the heavens, the square of the earth and the central point of unification. The first principle of the universe, the Tao, is identified with the centre, which is usually referred to in an inscription: 'May your eight sons and nine grandsons govern the centre.' Nine is the perfect number, made up of four females, *yin*, and five males, *yang*, represented by the moon and the sun.

If you ascend the T'ai Shan mountain, you will see the holy men; they eat the essence of jade and drink the limpid spring; they have attained the Way of Heaven; all things are in their natural state; they yoke the Hornless Dragon to their chariot; they mount the floating clouds; may you have high office and rank, may you preserve your sons and grandsons.

I Ching

Opposite The heavily-decorated reverse side of this ancient Chinese mirror resembles a mandala.

A Christian 'mandala'

the circle as an image for concentrating spiritual thought and feeling is omnipresent in Christianity, especially in its more mystical representations. It appears in the form of rose windows and in labyrinths, and is one obvious way of connecting the points of the cross, the basic symbol of the Christian religion. The cross itself is strongly associated with the idea of a crossroads at which essential energy is concentrated. It is also the Tree of Life, with its inevitable connotations of decay, death and rebirth. Significantly the circle in this 14th-century French miniature (*opposite*) is shown quartered by a cross, while angels turn the outer wheel of the universe, indicating that it is driven by the creative energy of God.

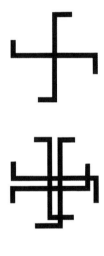

The hermetic universe

The obliteration of distinctions, the experience of the essential unity of the cosmos, and therefore of God, are concepts shared by the mystics of all the world's great religions. Such experience has, perhaps, played a smaller part in the rituals and liturgies of the West, mainly because the Christian Church has always interposed itself between the individual and direct experience of the supreme enlightenment. Nevertheless, certain figures and groups within the Western tradition – notably those associated with hermetic and kabbalistic beliefs and practices – have expressed the longing for the ultimate experience in diagrammatic mandala-like forms which incorporate archetypal symbols.

Opposite The endless circle is a symbol of the expanding universe, the cycle of repetition and renewal. In Robert Fludd's engraving of 1617, the outer circles of the diagram are those of supernatural fire filled with cherubim and seraphim, symbols of divine energy. Nature is shown as a naked woman, chained by her right wrist to God (represented as 'JHVH', Jahveh) and by her left to the monkey, symbol of lower nature.

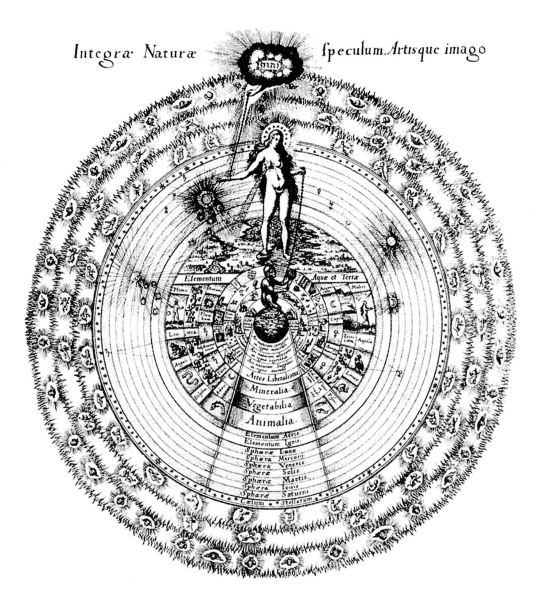

THE WAY TO THE GODS

The mandala is a compact mystical diagram, concentrating spiritual energy; it is an icon of religious experience and, at the same time, a visible manifestation of divinity. It is the dwelling place of the highest deity and often also of lesser deities. In Buddhist mandalas the Supreme Buddha may be shown wearing a mantle and royal tiara, denoting his status as Universal Monarch. In Tantric practices the diety may be represented by the *yantra,* a diagram of interlocking geometrical shapes.

This is the truth: as from a fire aflame thousands of sparks come forth, even so from the Creator an infinity of beings have life and to him return again.

But the spirit of light above form, never-born, within all, outside all, is in radiance above life and mind, and beyond this creation's Creator.

From him comes all life and mind, and the senses of all life. From him comes space and light, air and fire and water, and this earth that holds us all.

Mundaka Upanishad

The centre of this diagram of the cosmos, from 18th-century Rajasthan, India, takes the form of a maze-like swastika, a graphic representation of the journey the initiate must make to achieve a sense of being at one with the Supreme Being.

The outer triangles of this elaborate Shri Yantra from Nepal, *c.* 1700, are peopled with divinities representing the sub-divided forces of the Great Goddess, Shakti.

Shiva-Shakti

The most important and most universal Hindu *yantra* is the Shri Yantra, a complex arrangement of triangles and lotus leaves expressing the whole motive energy of the universe and the delicate balance of the male and female principles. The five inverted triangles symbolize Shakti, the female goddess representative of all in the cosmos that is active and creative; the four upright triangles symbolize Shiva, the male principle and supreme consciousness. How the triangles intersect is clearly open to interpretation, and the initiate may read them in a number of ways. However, the dualism is more apparent than real: what this *yantra* is expressing is the unity of the cosmic consciousness with which the individual can identify.

To the utterly at-one with Shiva there's no dawn, no new moon, no noonday, nor equinoxes, nor sunsets, nor full moons…

Devara Dasimayya

The god of the waters

hindu ceremonies and meditational rites to invoke
a divine essence require a round receptacle to be placed
in the centre of the mandala or *yantra*. This is filled with
various substances and is the receptacle in which the
deity will first lodge before passing into the supplicant.
Varuna, to whom this mandala is devoted, is the deity
of cosmic order and also the Lord of Waters.

**Now I shall speak of the *yantra* of the planets, which
promotes all kinds of peace... When one has
worshipped the planets... the eight Governors of the
directions should be worshipped... (including) Varuna,
god of the waters in the west, who is white, sits
on a Makara monster, holding a noose.**

Shiva in the *Mahanirvana Tantra*

A contemporary Varuna *yantra* from the holy city of
Benares, India; the outer enclosure is guarded by the
emblems of deities and regents.

Above and opposite The bodhisattvas, those figures of boundless compassion, have their own mandalas and *yantras* which take on the imagery of the cosmic 'whole' and may therefore be used for meditation and illumination. These *yantras* invoke the goddess Tara, one of the female bodhisattvas, whose name means 'she who causes one to cross', alluding to crossing over the turbulent river of existence to peace on the other side, Rajasthan, India, 18th century, gouache on paper.

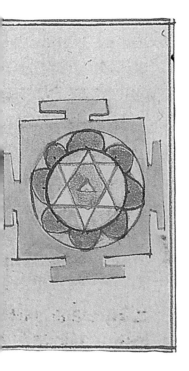

Few cross the river of time and are able
to reach nirvana. Most of them run up
and down only on this side of the river.

But those who when they know the law
follow the path of the law, they shall
reach the other shore and go beyond
the realm of death.

Leaving behind the path of darkness
and following the path of light, let the
wise man leave his home life and go into
a life of freedom. In solitude that few enjoy,
let him find his joy supreme: free from
possessions, free from desires and free
from whatever may darken his mind.

The Dhammapada

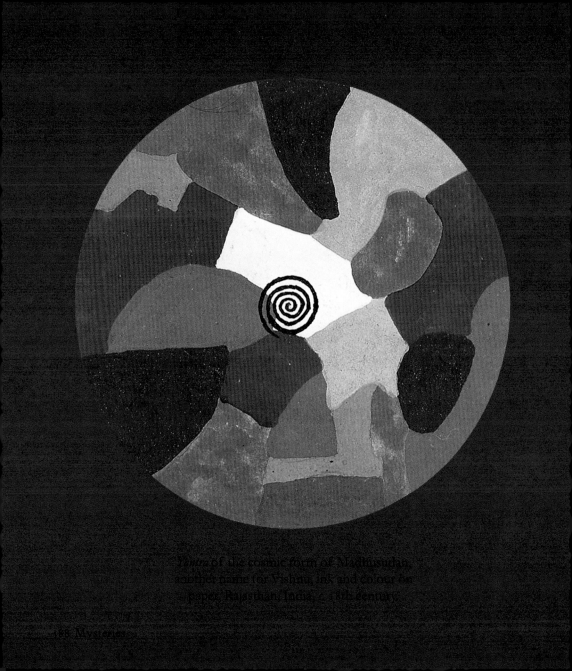

Yantra of the cosmic form of Madhusudan,
another name for Vishnu, ink and colour on
paper, Rajasthan, India, *c.* 18th century.

Vishnu

One of the great high gods of Hinduism, Vishnu
appears in a number of incarnations, including
Krishna, Rama and even the Buddha. He is the deity
worshipped by one of the major sects of Tantrists,
the Vaishnavas – the others are Shaivas (devotees
of Shiva) and Shaktas (followers of Shakti).
Legend has it that the sacred places of Tantric
worship were created on the sites where the parts
of Shakti fell to the ground after she had been
dismembered by Vishnu.

A goddess of abundance

an important monthly ritual of Nepalese Buddhism
is the worship of the bodhisattva Amoghapasa
Lokeshvara, the goddess of abundance, Vasundhara.
Suitably placated, she is responsible for well-being
and the prevention of poverty. In mandalas devoted
to specific deities, the god resides in the centre, also
known as the 'palace'. It has been suggested that this
form was originally inspired by the Mesopotamian
ziggurat, a pyramid-shaped terraced temple, which
was itself a cosmogram of the universe.

Opposite A Nepalese
16th-century painted
mandala to Vasundhara,
goddess of the earth
and plenty.

The Buddhas

the correspondence between the macrocosm and the microcosm in the mandalas of Tantric Buddhism is often expressed in forceful, figurative terms. Like the Hindu vision of the universe, Buddhism saw both external phenomena and internal experience in quinary terms: five elements, five colours, five objects of the senses and the five senses themselves. Vajrayana Buddhism sees the supreme original consciousness, Vajrasattva, as divided into five wisdom Buddhas: Vairocana, 'The Brilliant One'; Aksobhya, 'The Unshakable'; Ratnasambhava, 'The Matrix of the Jewel'; Amitabha, 'The Infinite Light', and Amoghasiddhi, 'The Infallible Realization'. Each one is associated with a particular colour, personality type and a passion or human shortcoming.

Opposite This 18th-century Tibetan *tanka* shows the mandalas of the peaceful Buddhas, the knowledge-holder Buddhas, the wrathful Buddhas, and of the Buddhas who preside over the realms of reincarnation.

Mandalas of the dead

The mandala reproduced opposite, (and the one that follows on p. 596), represent deities of the other world and are thus intended to both instruct the adept in the ways of death and help him prepare for his own departure. According to *The Tibetan Book of the Dead*, the newly deceased passes through a preliminary period of consideration during which he must face the 'lights of the six places of rebirth', which will eventually determine his fate. During this period the dead is confronted first by the benign Buddhas for seven days, and then by the wrathful ones.

By what earthly path could you entice the Buddha who, enjoying all, can wander through the pathless ways of the infinite? The Buddha who is awake, whose victory cannot be turned into defeat, and whom no one can conquer?

The Dhammapada

Opposite A 19th-century Tibetan mandala of the forty-two peaceful Buddhas and bodhisattvas.

The judgment

Opposite A 19th-century Tibetan mandala of the wrathful Buddhas: 'They are but the benevolent Buddhas and bodhisattvas, changed in their outward aspect. In you alone are the five wisdoms, the source of the benign spirits! In you alone are the five poisons, the source of the angry spirits! It is from your own mind therefore that all this has sprung.'

The Tibetan Book of the Dead

the initiate is now invited to reflect on the wrathful Buddhas and the judgment of the fourteenth day: 'You are now before Yama, King of the Dead. In vain will you try to lie, and to deny or conceal the evil deeds you have done. The Judge holds up before you the shining mirror of karma, wherein all your deeds are reflected. But again you have to deal with dream images, which you yourself have made and which you project outside, without recognizing them as your own work. The mirror in which Yama seems to read your past is your own memory, and also his judgment is your own. It is you yourself who pronounce your own judgment, which in its turn determines your next rebirth.'
The Tibetan Book of the Dead

The lotus mandala
of Shamvara

The mandala of Shamvara, or Paramasukha Chakrasamvara, shows the god with his female counterpart, Vajravarahi, immediately surrounded by four female Buddhas – Dakini, Lama, Khandarohi and Rupini. Between each figure is a cup made from a skull and full of blood, symbolizing an end to the disintegration of the world of nature and the human psyche and the recovery of primordial unity. The globular lotus of this mandala opens into eight petals, the first of three rings of eight elements.

Even the gods long to be like the Buddhas who are awake and watch, who find peace in contemplation and who, calm and steady, find joy in renunciation.

The Dhammapada

Opposite A three-dimensional Tibetan-Chinese mandala to invoke Shamvara, the Supreme Bliss Wheel Integration Buddha, in gilt-bronze, 17th century.

An 18th-century gilt-brass offering mandala from northern China.

Mount Meru –
an offering mandala

The inner surface of the Tantric mandala is first divided by two main lines, the *brahma sutra*, from north to south, and from east to west. At the intersection of the two lines is Mount Meru, the *axis mundi* at the centre of the horizontal plane of the mandala and also the equivalent of the median canal in the human body. Three-dimensional mandalas were sometimes made in dough for the ritual of offering to Mount Meru. These were not so much aids to meditation as direct communication with the axial centre of the world, surrounded by the four continents of the Indian cosmology: crescent-shaped Purva Videha in the east; triangular Jambudvipa in the south; circular Apara Godaniya in the west, and the square Uttara Kuru in the north.

FROM DARKNESS
TO LIGHT

The mandala is an external support for meditation; it helps provoke the feelings and visions by which one can arrive at a sense of unity within oneself and with the universe outside. This impulse towards a sense of being at one with the whole of nature can be favourably guided by the arrangement in solid form of rays, flowers, circles and squares, and the representations of gods and goddesses. Thus, the original impulse to find a formal support for the deepest spiritual feelings may become in itself a means of leading the whole man or woman towards the discovery of his or her secret reality and true illumination.

This 19th-century mandala makes a strong play of colour and form to draw the individual through meditation to a state of heightened consciousness.

Through meditation the adept must find himself or herself
at one with the still point of the *bindu*; this wooden example
from Andhra Pradesh, India wonderfully exemplifies the
feeling of movement to and from the centre.

Bindu

tantric belief finds the most concentrated point of the universe and the ultimate goal of the individual in the *bindu*. This is the centre of the circle, the irreducible point from which everything is directed; it is one of the two keys to the mandala – the other being the polarities. The *bindu* has neither beginning nor end and is neither positive nor negative; it is the embodiment of psychic and spiritual totality. It also suggests the waves of vibration from the centre; the more the form is in flux, the more it becomes whole.

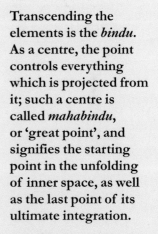

Transcending the elements is the *bindu*. As a centre, the point controls everything which is projected from it; such a centre is called *mahabindu*, or 'great point', and signifies the starting point in the unfolding of inner space, as well as the last point of its ultimate integration.

Giuseppe Tucci, *The Theory and Practice of the Mandala*

In the light of his vision he has found his freedom: his thoughts are peace, his words are peace and his work is peace.

The Dhammapada

The mandala of Aksobhya

the microcosmic structure of the mandala reflects the five components of the human personality: matter, sensation, motion, karma and cognizance. Each of these is associated with a colour: white, yellow, red, green and dark blue respectively, which in turn profoundly affect the reading of a mandala. The principle of five is constant throughout the mandala; in this example (*opposite*) Aksobhya, one of the five cosmic Buddhas, is seated in its centre, with the other four gods around him. Outside the circle are the bodhisattvas.

In many schools of Buddhism the correspondence between macrocosm and microcosm is expressed in other terms. The five Buddhas do not remain remote divine forms in distant heavens, but descend into us. I am the cosmos and the Buddhas are in myself. In me is the cosmic light, a mysterious presence, even if it be obscured by error. But these five Buddhas are nevertheless in me, they are the five constituents of the human personality.

Giuseppe Tucci, *The Theory and Practice of the Mandala*

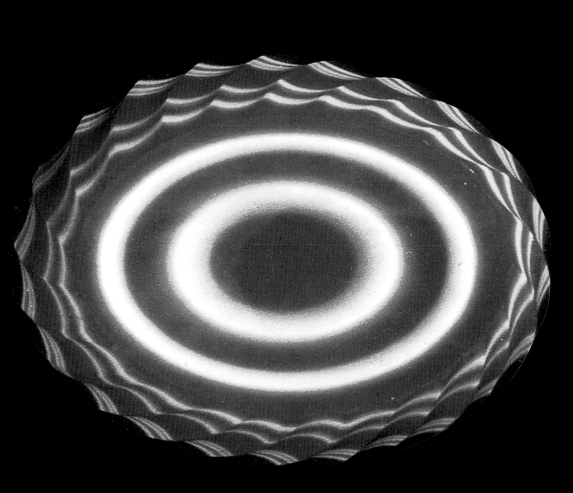

A stone from Rajasthan, India; the markings
resemble the orbital curves used to represent
the cosmos in certain forms of mandala.

A natural mandala

The adept who discovers natural phenomena incorporating the concentric rings of the classic mandala may also use them as aids to meditation and spiritual self-discovery. But the ability to recognize the mandala innate in the world outside and its symbolic significance is often the result of a long and patient apprenticeship to eradicate the ignorance which prevents us from seeing the truth of ourselves and the cosmos.

Arise! Watch. Walk on the right path. He who follows the right path has joy in this world and in the world beyond.

The Dhammapada

Serial meditation

The reading of the mandala is a progression, a stage by stage process of illuminating those areas of the consciousness that correspond to the parts of the world diagram. Step by step one must move from the outer circle of his or her being to successive interior states, aided by the movement from the perimeter of the mandala to sectors closer to the central point. While the experience yielded may differ from mandala to mandala, from *yantra* to *yantra*, the central point of complete catharsis cannot be represented as being other than what it is. And so the adept may meditate on a series of mandalas, realizing the various truths expressed by the different patterns, but always moving towards the spiritual fulfilment of the centre.

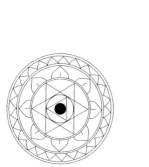

Opposite A Nepalese *tanka* painted with nine *yantras*, to be meditated on in series, ink and colour on paper, *c.* 19th century.

An 18th-century diagram from Himachal Pradesh,
India, used for computing astronomical periods, but
also as an aid to meditation, ink and colour on paper.

The makeshift mandala

the achievement of wholeness at the centre of an individual's being can be aided by virtually any phenomenon or diagram that provokes the appropriate forms of meditation. In Tantra the creative process of worship may be focused by diagrammatic forms initially intended for other purposes. These can be permanent, for long-term use; others are ephemeral, perhaps in sand or mud, to be destroyed after their immediate use as meditational icons. There does persist a belief, however, that a power diagram used over a long period accrues special significance and potency of its own.

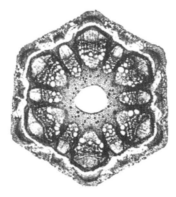

The yogi and his symbols

Opposite An 18th-century representation from Rajasthan, India of various systems and forms which can be used by the adept to comprehend the world and its structures. One's whole body must be brought into harmonious accord with the five elements, the *panchabhuta* of the cosmos: earth, fire, air, water and ether. In this diagram a beginner has yet to embark upon his journey of self-liberation – a state symbolized by his bound hands.

the choice for the initiate of aids to lead him or her to a full comprehension of the cosmos is wide indeed, from mandalas and *yantras* of varying complexity, to pentacles, swastikas and calligraphic diagrams. Once the neophyte has achieved catharsis, finding himself at one with whatever cosmic representation he is using, then he has access to total knowledge, even if only for a moment. Beyond and above the earthly plane is the Vajradhara, the absolute, at which point the mandala may be transferred into the mystic's own body.

An 18th-century Nepalese *yantra* intended to aid the
adept in the journey towards man-cosmos unity.

Man-cosmos unity

both Buddhism and Hinduism place great emphasis on the point of self-realization when the mandala or *yantra* of the external world leads to the mandala of the individual. The symbols of the original mandala are now arranged in a similar form within the body. Ideally, the new centre of the mandala should be the *brahmarandhra*, the 'cavity of Brahma' at the top of the head, the termination of the median canal which runs along the spinal column. This columnar structure is the equivalent to the central mountain of the universe around which are arranged the various celestial planes, themselves the equivalents of the various centres of the human body (*chakras*).

Leave the past behind; leave the future behind; leave the present behind. Thou art then ready to go to the other shore. Never more shalt thou return to a life that ends in death.

The Dhammapada

The chakras

according to the Buddhist teaching we are *bodhi* and *dharmakaya*, 'Buddha essence'; the Hindu adept directs himself or herself towards Shiva, the 'Supreme Consciousness'. The force which moves through us – the principle of awakening – is seen as a luminous point ascending through five stages from the perineum to the *brahmarandhra*. The light is equivalent to the Light of the World, the everlasting origin of all things; it moves in the centre of the individual, just as the centre of the external mandala symbolizes the first principle of the cosmos.

Opposite and right Ink and gouache scroll-paintings of *chakras*, from Rajasthan, India, *c.* 17th century.

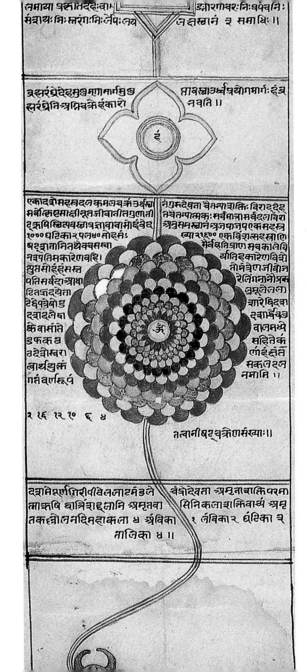

A late 19th-century representation from Rajasthan, India of the *chakras*, with the full flowering of the Kundalini principle shown above the head.

The subtle body

the fusion of the individual with the universal, the awakening of the whole body as a reflection of the world of time and space, is the object of Kundalini yoga. This meditative discipline concentrates on the awakening of the coiled Kundalini, the female energy that must be awoken to unite finally with Shiva, the pure consciousness of the whole cosmos. When Kundalini is awakened she progresses like a serpent up through the seven *chakras*, the centres of consciousness in the body that may function as inner mandalas, until she reaches the seventh, *sahasrara chakra*, the seat of the absolute (Shiva-Shakti).

A man should control his words and mind and should not do any harm with his body. If these ways of action are pure he can make progress on the path of the wise.

The Dhammapada

The transcendent realm

As the Kundalini force ascends the seven *chakras* of the subtle body, the adept may meditate on each of the power centres, either in its own right or with the aid of an external mandala or *yantra*. The sixth *chakra*, seated between the eyebrows, is known as *ajna*; its associated element is the mind itself, represented as a circle with two petals and an inverted triangle. Of particular importance is its seed mantra, which is the most powerful of all sounds, the primordial vibration OM.

When all the subtle channels of the body meet, like spokes in the centre of a wheel, there he moves in the heart and transforms his one form into many. Upon OM, Atman, your self, place your meditation. Glory unto you in your far-away journey beyond darkness!

Mundaka Upanishad

In the iconography of Tantric Buddhism the *chakras* may be represented as highly visual mandalas in their own right; from the power circles of the subtle body stretches a network of channels and energy centres, represented here in a 17th-century Nepalese image of the adept in a transcendent state.

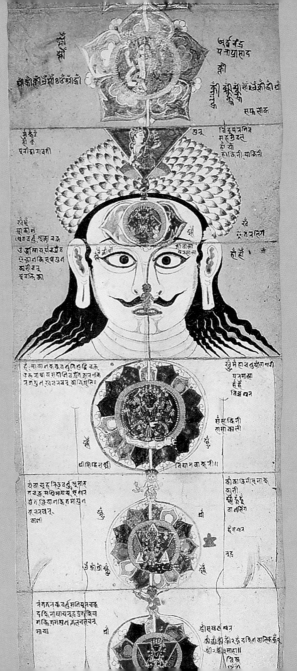

Mantra

While meditating on the mandala, the postulant, *sadhaka*, will intone a mantric sound, syllables based on sound vibrations, which parallel the stages of understanding of the cosmos and the awakening of the *chakras* of the subtle body. The most potent of all mantras is the sound OM, the representation of universal knowledge. With two other syllables, AH and HUM, associated respectively with the throat and the heart, it makes up the three Diamond Seeds, which introduce the divine essence into the body. This transfer is realized by the placing of the hand on the appropriate part of the body as the syllable is intoned.

OM. This eternal word is all: what was, what is and what shall be, and what beyond is in eternity. All is OM.

Mandukya Upanishad

Opposite 'Monarch of all sounded things': an 18th-century *yantra* from Rajasthan, India expressing the power of the syllable OM.

THE WAY FORWARD

As a diagram of the cosmos, as a representation of our sense of wholeness and of oneness with the rest of the universe, the mandala has relevance and meaning way beyond the liturgies of Hinduism and Buddhism. People of widely differing cultures and historic periods have been drawn to the universality of its circular form, as well as its unique power to satisfy a longing for perfection.

When all desires that cling to the heart disappear, then a mortal becomes immortal, and even in this life attains liberation.

The Upanishads:
The Supreme Teaching

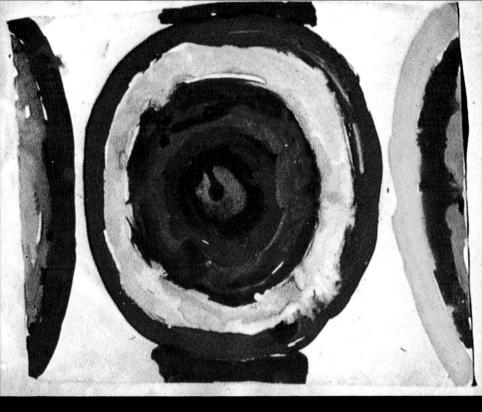

This image – created after children had been in
silent meditation for a short time and were then

The golden flower

as a means of inner healing and self-orientation, the mandala form has passed from east to west. The famous analytical psychiatrist C. G. Jung noted the form as one of the archetypal symbols issuing from the collective unconscious; as a representation of man's need for wholeness and perfection it could be used as a therapeutic device in the reintegration of shattered personalities. Individual symbols and visions could be accommodated within the form to concentrate fruitful meditation, leading to a proper awareness of self in relation to the world without.

Opposite Mandalas drawn by a female patient of C. G. Jung.

Astral doorways

The fascination which the mandala and *yantra* forms held for Jung and his disciples was not the only example of the West adopting these Eastern forms. Symbols derived from these Tantric aids to meditation and the achievement of altered states of consciousness have long been valued by devotees of the occult. Tattva cards, a set of twenty-five coloured symbols, were used extensively by members of the Order of the Golden Dawn, a Western occult organization founded in the 19th-century, as aids to visionary experience.

Sacred Sex

A SEXUAL UNIVERSE

Most creation myths refer to the beginning of the world in terms of mating and fertilization, since sexual congress is the image most readily available to human beings to explain their origins. The book of Genesis sees the emergence of humankind through the original parents, Adam and Eve. The Homeric water god Oceanus mates with his sister, the water goddess Tethys, to produce three thousand sons. In Orphic literature, Night is impregnated by Wind and lays a silver egg, the Orphic or Cosmic Egg; the first-born god hatched from the egg is Eros, the god of love. Sky and earth matings have often inspired the fertility rituals of the religions and mythologies of the world; in the ancient Egyptian story of Nut and Geb, the couple are brother and sister, but from their union sprang all living things.

Opposite A traditional Tantric painting of the phallus; the rounded forms also suggest the primal egg of creation.

Cosmic Egg

The egg, outcome of sexual congress and fertilization, is a perfect symbol of creation, notably dominant in Egyptian, Polynesian, Japanese, Indian and Mesoamerican creation mythology. In certain Indian beliefs the primal egg (Brahmanda) separated into two halves, one of gold, the heavens, and one of silver, the earth. From this same egg, the primordial, androgynous man, Prajapati, also emerged. In Mithraic belief, widespread among the soldiers of the Roman army, the central god Mithras sprang armed from an egg, releasing the forces from which the cosmos developed.

Above Egg-shaped stone with markings thought in Tantric cults to represent the penetrating, fertilizing powers of the phallus.

Opposite The egg-birth of the god Mithras, originally a Vedic creation god whose cult spread to Persia and eventually to the Roman Empire; this relief, which shows the god surrounded by the twelve signs of the Zodiac is from Housesteads Fort along Hadrian's Wall, England, 2nd century AD.

Primal womb

although many of the world's greatest belief systems see the cosmos as being formed of the interaction of primeval forces and therefore suitably symbolized by sexual congress, the actual creation of the world is often denoted by reference to the womb and to the female principle. Even Shiva, the supreme male consciousness of Hinduism, is activated by Shakti, the feminine power and the original womb – *matrix* in Latin – of the universe. In alchemy, both Arabic and Western, all matter (*prima materia*) was viewed as a manifestation of the primeval womb, *mater* (mother) and *matrix*. In Taoism, the feminine *yin* is regarded as the all-pervading way of the cosmos.

Opposite Mount Meru, symbol of the origin of the universe and the primal womb, gouache on paper, Rajasthan, India, 18th century.

Below The Cosmic Woman, of whom all things and beings are born; Brahma the Creator reposes in her *yoni* (vulva), and she is crowned by Shiva, gouache, Rajasthan, India, 18th century.

Sacred Sex 641

Sexual balance

according to many systems of belief, once the cosmos had emerged from primordial chaos, born of the confluence of two forces or principles, it was subject to a process of order-making. This was often seen to be achievable by the conjunction of opposites, as in the inseparability of *purusha* (male) and *prakriti* (female) energies in Hinduism. The sexual act is the supreme symbol of this desire for balance in the universe.

Opposite Purusha and *prakriti* represented in human form; their conjunction in the sexual act symbolized the primordial male-female balance, gouache on paper, Orissa, India, 17th century.

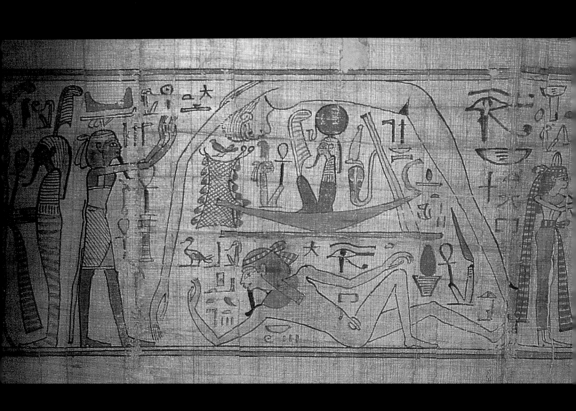

Earth and sky

Identification of the procreators of the cosmos is central to most ancient mythologies and religions. Among the Navajo of the southwest United States the couple are simply known as Mother Earth and Father Sky. The association of the earth with the female figure is reinforced by her portrayal with the fruits and produce of the earth. Most other traditions ascribe female qualities to the earth; in Taoism the *yin* qualities of the terrestrial plane are seen as being penetrated by *yang* influences from the heavens, such as rain falling. Unusually, the ancient Egyptians symbolized the earth by a masculine being, Geb, who showed an unnatural affection for his sister, the sky goddess Nut. The relationship between heaven and earth is a universal theme in many ancient legends of fertility.

Opposite Geb and Nut, the brother and sister progenitors of the ancient Egyptian universe, separated by the barque of Re, burial painting, papyrus, 1000 BC.

Serpent

representations of the serpent or of similar reptilian beasts, such as the dragon, have wound their way through the mythologies of the world since time immemorial. Once the conditions for creation have happened, then various forces, often strongly sexual, come into play, and the serpent symbolizes many of these. In the Christian bible, it is the incarnation of the Devil. In Tantra, the serpent Kundalini is the feminine embodiment of the material and spiritual energy in man, eventually rising from her position at the base of the spine to awaken the nerve centres of the body.

Above A yogini with serpentine energy protruding from her *yoni*, wood, southern India, *c.* 1800.

Opposite A Tantric painting of serpents, symbols of cosmic energy, coiled around an invisible *lingam*.

Left An Aztec terracotta figure, *c.* 1500; the sun disc between the figure's thighs symbolizes fertility.

Below Bronze Age drawing of a male figure with a solar disc attached to his phallus, Camonica Valley, Italy.

Sun...

most magnificent of the visible heavenly bodies – bringer of light, heat and energy – how powerful a symbol the sun must have seemed to the ancient peoples of the earth. For the peoples of Mesoamerica it was another embodiment of the male principle, associated with kingship and solar animals, such as the jaguar and eagle. The Incas considered the sun as their divine male ancestor, while the Aztecs believed they lived under the government of the Fifth Sun. Bronze Age carvings in Europe have been found that associate the disc of the sun with phallic figurines.

In alchemy the conjunction of Sol, the masculine sun, and Luna, the feminine moon, is viewed as a union of soul and body, gold and silver, and king and queen.

Above The sun represented in a 15th-century Italian manuscript of *De Sphaera*; in astrology the sun represents the essential self of man.

...and moon

Characterized by the 16th-century historian of the Incas, Garcilaso de la Vega, as the 'wife of the sun', the moon has traditionally been seen as distinctly feminine. In ancient societies the brighter sun was appropriated by the dominant male sex, although the ancient Egyptians ascribed the goddess Nut to the sun and described the moon as the 'sun shining at night'. Chinese tradition saw the intercourse of Fuxi (sun) and Nuwa (moon) as symbolizing fecundity and renewal. In Roman mythology, the moon is associated with the goddess Diana, the huntress.

Above The astrological moon in the *De Sphaera* manuscript, Italy, 15th century.

Opposite Fuxi and Nuwa represent the sun and moon in Taoist creation myths.

Sexual landscapes

Below A relief figure of a tree spirit, pink sandstone, India, n.d.

the principle of creation as the interaction of two forces could often be seen in the land formations of the earth as the ancient peoples came to terms with their environment. The produce of the earth – resulting from the intervention of sun and rain gods – nourished them. Even the very shapes of mountain and tree, valley and lake, phallus and vulva, indicated that the primal act of creation was a continuing symbol system which explained man's relationship to the universe. Thousands of people still visit the two Meoto-iwa (wedded rocks) at Futamigaura in Japan, which represent a legendary Japanese husband and wife, from whose union all of the Japanese islands were created. The sacred ropes that run from one to the other symbolize the unity of the cosmos.

The Garden of Eden,
Hugo van der Goes,
c. 1467-8.

In the garden of good and evil

Detail from a bronze door at the Cathedral of Hildesheim, Germany, showing Adam and Eve before God, *c.* 1015.

The process of bringing order to the newly-born cosmos resulted in its own potent sexual symbolism. In ancient Persian and Egyptian cultures the garden, arranged around a central pool of water, symbolized control over the natural world. For Christians, the Garden of Eden is the location of humankind's original sin, where the serpent – symbol of base sensuality – led Adam and Eve to eat the forbidden fruit from the Tree of Knowledge.

Cosmic twins

As the cosmos in ancient cultures was regarded as the product of a duality, many societies naturally found the idea of twins sexually ambiguous. In certain African cultures one of the twins was killed immediately after birth since it was imagined the pair had indulged in sexual debauchery in the womb. A more positive view of twins, however, is taken by the Dogon people of Mali who believe that humanity sprang from multiple pairs of twins who were half human and half serpent. The Gemini sign of the Zodiac is represented by twins – symbolizing duality and separation, contradiction and similarity – as the constellation's brightest stars are named for the mythical brothers Castor and Pollux.

Above Stone image expressing the cosmic duality; from one side it appears as a nursing mother, and from the other side as an erect phallus.

Opposite Male/female double-face mask expressing the duality of nature and society, Ivory Coast.

GODDESS

The female principle of the universe is expressed in many forms: earth mother, virgin, seductress, bringer of plenty, but also avenger. From ancient Mesopotamia to the peoples of Mesoamerica, the original, ever-fecund goddess of the universe has been worshipped and revered. The theme of the great mother runs through the literature of Hinduism as Shakti, goddess and universal creator, to Christianity, in which the Madonna is the protectress. In creation myths the goddess is the female partner in the great cosmic act of love which resulted in the birth of the earth and its peoples, and she is the benefactress of the harvest and of fertility.

Opposite left A Mayan fertility figure in the form of a pregnant woman.

Opposite right Statuette of the earth goddess, the essence of fecundity, Mesopotamia, 4th century BC.

The goddess is also potentially a lover: the Greek goddess of love, Aphrodite, (Venus to the Romans), as a femme fatale, looks out from an enclosed garden, while men look on with desire. The detail is from a French 15th-century illuminated manuscript, *Les Échecs amoureux*.

Vulva

The power of the female half of creation
was expressed for many ancient peoples
by the form of the vulva. For the ancient
Taoist, natural clefts, valleys and concave
land formations suggesting the female
genitals were indicative of powerful *yin*
essences. In Tantra the *yoni* is represented
as a downward-turned triangle, suggesting
the form of pubic hair. This triangle,
however, is rarely seen alone; the symbol
is likely to be depicted with the Tantric
phallic symbol to indicate the persistent
duality of the male and female forces.
In the ancient male-dominated societies
of Mesoamerica the vulva was considered
to be a fount of great magical power.

Opposite A panel
depicting the four
stages of woman's
life; the goddess in
the upper right
quarter is dressed as
a man, but is shown
projecting magic
power from her
vulva, Mexico,
Mixtec period.

Below A Tantric *yoni*
symbol.

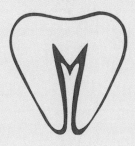

Virgin

a contrast to the earth mother – the all-protective female figure – is the virgin, symbol of purity and godliness. In the West the idea that virginity is a condition for closeness to God has been amply reinforced by the biblical account of the virgin birth of Christ. Yet numerous diverse cultures have also associated important figures with virgin births, including the Greek hero Perseus, Alexander the Great, Gengis Khan, Lao Tzu and the Aztec god Quetzalcoatl.

Numerous cultures venerate the purity of pubescent girls; in certain Tantric sects they are worshipped as the early incarnation of the mother goddess. This is recalled in the Hindu festival of Durga Puja when young girls are dressed in new clothes and worshipped by their families.

An 18th-century Indian painting of a naked girl adorned with jewels, image of the young mother goddess; the two birds with her are symbols of the liberated soul.

Female initiation

The idea of initiation dates from the earliest societies and is continued in our own: the process of a human being acquiring the secrets of the universe through the passage to adulthood. For many peoples the onset of menstruation signifies this transition in women, putting a woman in touch with the flow of the great female energies of the universe. Among Tantric sects this is seen as the introduction of the woman to the fundamental processes of nature; the resultant blood is sometimes venerated, to the extent of being drunk ritually with wine. Many African peoples have elaborate initiation ceremonies, during which the initiates will receive the traditional knowledge of the older women of the community. Menstruation rites are often associated with the fertile moon cycle and are also related to the cycle of the harvest.

Above Seated figure from Sierra Leone, representing a woman who has just completed initiation into a women's association.

Opposite A puberty initiation ceremony, Ghana.

Birth and rebirth

Below Human birth
as symbol of
universal creation,
wood carving,
southern India,
c. 18th century.

$f$rom the ancient Celts to the
peoples of Asia and those of
Mesoamerica, the act of giving
birth was seen as a symbol of
renewal and also of creation itself.
Sacred femininity was regarded at
its most intense as a new being was
pushed out into the world. In
Tantric tradition the most intense
awakening, the fullest expression
of the Kundalini force, is the act of
giving birth which sets in motion
again the cosmic cycle of birth,
death, rebirth and renewal.

Opposite Leaf from an Aztec codex,
showing the rebirth of the god
Quetzalcoatl after his journey through the
underworld; the two figures at the foot of
the painting symbolize the reborn god.

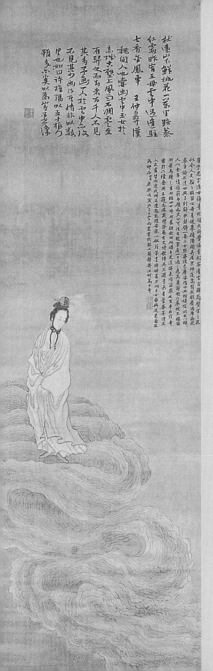

Above Soapstone seal showing Lan Tsai-ho walking among clouds, Ch'ing Dynasty, China, late 17th century.

Opposite A jade lady talisman to concentrate *yin* essences.

The jade lady

though the sexual and spiritual force of
the female underlies much of the deepest
symbolism of all cultures, every system
of belief has its own particular version.
The jade lady of Taoism, Lan Tsai-ho, is
portrayed in swirling lines suggestive of
organic forms and therefore of the *yin*
essences of the world. Her association
with jade – regarded as the solidified
semen of the dragon – is potent indeed.
Jade is the mineral symbol of the congress
of the celestial dragon and the elements
of the earth, the most perfect expression
of the union of *yin* and *yang* and
therefore of the interpenetration
of the two great universal forces.

Sphinx

although the term 'sphinx' is commonly associated with the monumental statuary of ancient Egypt, portraying a being with the head of a king and the body of a lion, there is another entirely different tradition from ancient Greece. It expresses the sinister side of the female force, often in disturbing imagery in the form of a demon-like winged woman, lying in wait for passers-by to whom she poses certain riddles. Those who cannot disentangle her webs of meaning she devours. Only Oedipus succeeded in this game of life and death, symbolizing the rite of passage which each being must undergo to perceive the truths of the universe.

Above Stone figure of a sphinx from a Roman cemetery, Colchester, England, 1st century AD.

Opposite The Kiss of the Sphinx, Franz von Stuck, *c.* 1895.

Kali

Opposite Devi, the great female principle, of which Kali is a form, with a severed head denoting the end of one cosmic cycle, and the waters of Shiva which symbolize the start of the new.

Below The figure of Kali seated on the corpse of Shiva, sculpture, Bengal, 18th century.

the manifestations of the Hindu goddess Kali as the embodiment of the feminine force are many. She is the Shakti of Shiva, his feminine component and the begetter of life, but may also imply death when she takes the form of the goddess Durga. As supreme goddess, Kali is most widely worshipped as the giver of life and, potentially, also its destroyer. In her benevolent aspect, she may be represented in holy nakedness, full-breasted. Yet so complete a figure is she that she may also inspire terror, the form of the goddess which leapt forth from the brow of Durga to take victory in the battle between the divine and anti-divine and establish Devi, the world female power.

A red-figure water jug
depicting the death of
Actaeon, *c.* 375–350 BC.

Diana

The goddess of the hunt in Roman mythology (Artemis in Greek mythology) is herself symbol and allegory of the feminine force, associated with virginity and independence from men. Her personal symbols are the crescent moon and the bow and arrows. Her dislike of male attention is embodied in the tale of Actaeon who, having spied on the goddess bathing, was transformed into a stag and torn to pieces by his own hunting dogs. A more hidden aspect of Diana, indicative of her power as a feminine icon, was her adoption in the 19th century as a central cult figure in witchcraft.

THE MALE PRINCIPLE

O ften associated with the heavens in mythologies in which the cosmos is the outcome of celestial and terrestrial copulation, the male as god, hero or buffoon has continued to provide a significant counterpoint in iconography and symbolism to the image of the all-giving, fecund goddess.

In Western cultures the male archetypes are often sexually aggressive: the Greek and Roman gods, the lustful satyr and the all-conquering hero. But there are other, gentler traditions: the saint who resists the lure of fleshy temptation; the Grail knight, courtly in his love, who searches for the beatific vision of the holy Christian vessel, symbol of the wholeness of the world.

Opposite A yogic carving in rock crystal of a phallic form; the smoothness of the rounded lines suggest, too, that this object was intended to represent the egg, original source of creation, 18th century.

Gods

Two representations of the myth of Leda and the swan: a Roman copy of an original Greek sculpture *(below)*, and a painting after Michelangelo, after 1530 *(opposite)*.

When Hamlet compared man to a god he was associating mere mortals with the embodiment of the grandest, most powerful forces of the universe. Every ancient society and many modern has had its gods, deities of localized or even supreme power, the driving forces of the male principle. In the Greek mythology Zeus, king of the gods (known as Jupiter to the Romans), replaced his father Cronos (Saturn in the Roman tale), embodiment of early chaos, to become the figurehead of universal order. His supreme position was underlined by imperious sexual conquest in various guises: as a shower of gold he impregnated Danäe; as a bull he carried away Europa; and as a swan he seduced Leda.

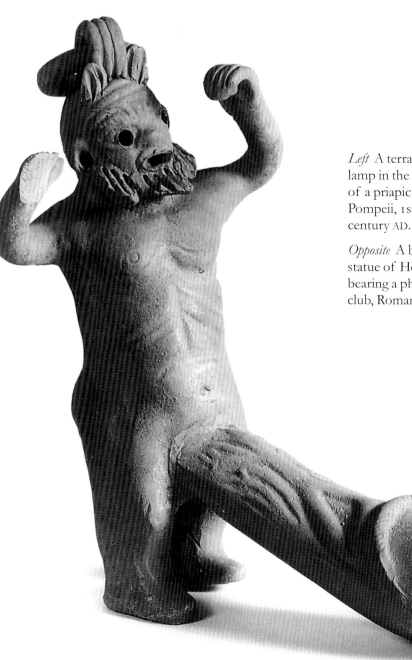

Left A terracotta lamp in the form of a priapic hero, Pompeii, 1st century AD.

Opposite A bronze statue of Hercules bearing a phallic club, Roman, n.d.

Heroes

In many mythologies there exists a class of powerful male beings, not quite gods, yet quasi-celestial in that they are often the sons of gods, embodying the universal principle of penetration of the earth by the forces of the heavens. Hercules, the hero of the Twelve Labours, was the son of Jupiter and the mortal woman Alcmena, and was eventually poisoned by his jealous wife Dejanira. As Hercules prepared to die, grasping his faithful phallic club, Jupiter rescued him by decreeing that only the mother's mortal half of Hercules should die. Jupiter took up the remaining, divine part of his son to give him a place among the gods.

Satyrs

demons of nature, half-man, half-beast, these mythological creatures express an important aspect of male sexuality. In classical tradition they are associated with the god Pan and are characterized by insatiable sexual appetites. Satyrs are also associated with the Greek god Dionysus (Bacchus to the Romans), god of wine and seducer of nymphs. Such masculine expressions of nature spirits are perhaps related to the idea of untutored chaos, before the balancing of male and female forces brought order to the cosmos.

Above A satyr-like figure portrayed on a Greek coin from the island of Naxos.

Opposite A lustful satyr uncovers Venus, *Pardo Venus*, Titian, *c.* 1540.

Phallus

Below A low-relief
phallic amulet,
Roman, *c.* 2nd
century AD.

Below A low-relief
phallic amulet,
Roman, *c.* 2nd
century AD.

Opposite An Indian
carving of the youth
Shiva conducting
self- fellatio.

Celebration of this supreme symbol
of male power, the cult of the phallus
attracted adherents throughout the
world, from southeast Asia to the
western reaches of the Celtic lands.
Among Indian sects, the cult of the
lingam parallels that of the *yoni*; the
representation of the sexual organ is
often highly stylized, rendered as such a
large-scale column that it may be taken
as an *axis mundi* or pillar of the world,
and an affirmation of male power.
Ancient Greek and Roman art is rich in
phallic figures in which it is possible to
discern a certain element of secular
jollity, especially in the images of the
god Priapus, the Greek god of fertility
who is usually depicted with an
oversized phallus.

Male initiation

In societies and religions with a powerful shamanistic element the ceremonies of initiation occupy a special role. Among the Plains Indians of North America young initiates were sent out from the village to a remote place to experience the rigours of the environment, symbolizing their passage to manhood. Many other societies have traditionally regarded circumcision as the crucial rite of passage to male power. The word 'initiation', after all, indicates a beginning, a new awareness of the real secrets of the universe and of superior truths not discernible by a child. Modern Western society retains significant initiation rites as, for instance, in fraternal organizations such as Freemasonry.

Above A painted stool used in circumcision rituals by the Dogon people of Mali.

Opposite An Egyptian tomb relief showing a circumcision ceremony.

Left Detail of triptych, *The Temptation of St Anthony*, showing the saint in meditation, Hieronymus Bosch, *c.* 1500.

Opposite The flight from temptation: a 13th-century French miniature showing an initiate being inducted into the monastic life.

Temptation

Male power has not always been characterized by brute strength and sexual prowess. Another tradition, common in East and West, sees the strength of the male in ascetic isolation, proof of his strength to resist feminine wiles. In such beliefs sexual congress may be seen as temptation, virtually synonymous with evil, and – in the Judaeo-Christian world – symbolized by the entry of the serpent into the garden. St Anthony the Great

(AD 251–356) led an exemplary life of prayer and meditation in seclusion in the wilderness. The Devil saw such a life as an affront and tempted St Anthony by sending him beautiful and lascivious women. The saint resisted such blandishments and is seen as a symbol of restraint before the delights of the flesh. St Anthony is also considered to be the father of the Christian monastic tradition.

Castration

fear of emasculation appears in many cultures as a sign of fundamental insecurity in the male principle. The ancient Greek god Ouranos was castrated and his sexual organ thrown into the sea, from which a white foam arose to give birth to Aphrodite, goddess of love. The handsome young Anatolian shepherd Attis castrated himself in a mad frenzy of passion for the fertility goddess Cybele. His death inspired a quasi-religious cult whose followers exercised self-mutilation and deposited their genitals at shrines devoted to Attis. These legends seem to represent a side of masculinity free from association with a brute sexual force.

Above A bronze Roman statuette of Attis dancing, n.d.

A Roman sculpture of Attis transfigured, 2nd century AD; after castration, death and rebirth, the shepherd boy symbolizes the liberated soul, no longer burdened with sexual desire and anxiety.

SEX AND REDEMPTION

The sexual act is widely celebrated as a means of symbolizing and of achieving a state of grace. For the Taoist, successful sexual congress is one of the central symbols of the balancing of *yin* and *yang* forces, and therefore of harmony in the universe. In some Western traditions, the hermaphrodite, through the presence of both female and male, represents a wholeness and a resolution of the world's antagonisms. The garden, too, is a potent image of a happy state, a memory of a time before the intrusion of sin and the serpent into Eden. Some related traditions acknowledge a sexuality unfettered by cumbersome social conventions as the key to the holy joy evoked in Lucas Cranach's vision of *The Golden Age* (page 716).

Opposite The redemptive power of sex in Tantric practice and belief, whereby physical union following the proper disciplines lifts the participants to a higher spiritual plane, gouache, *c.* 1850.

Krishna and the gopis

for agricultural communities ritual dance was a means of ensuring the continuing beneficence of the heavens and the fertility of the earth. The dance celebrates the unity of existence, a quasi-sexual celebration of universal harmony and the balance between male and female forces. In the Hindu Ras Lila dance the love god Krishna couples successively with his cow-girl followers, the *gopis*. Before the dance begins, the *gopis'* clothes are stolen, leaving them naked before the flute-playing god who so charms them that each one believes she is dancing alone with him.

Above The stealing of the *gopis'* saris while the cow-girls are bathing, gouache, Calcutta, India, 19th century.

Opposite An embroidered muslin wedding cloth showing Krishna dancing with the *gopis*, Punjab, India, 18th century.

Shiva

although Shiva is undoubtedly the masculine absolute, his manifestations through the sign of the *lingam* are indicative of the reconciliation of the dual forces at work in the world. The column of the *lingam* is a symbol of the divine; contemplation of it revives the soul. It is usually, however, represented with the *yoni*, female symbol of the material and visible. Together the two constitute the Shiva-lingam, the unity of the visible and invisible, as well as the divine and the earthly.

Right A brass cover in the form of the *lingam-yoni*; two cobras protect the phallic head of Shiva while a third lies along the passage of the *yoni*.

Opposite Lingam-yoni, Allahabad, India.

Yin and yang

Simply put, the *yin* and *yang* of Taoism represent the opposition of two cosmic principles. The *yin* is the feminine principle, characterized by receptivity, humidity, shadow and earth; the *yang* is masculine, representing the heavens, dryness, prominent forms and the Emperor. The coupling of the two, and therefore the achievement of harmony, is readily symbolized by the sexual act. The intertwined symbols of *yin* and *yang* are surrounded by a circle, indicative of the primal wholeness of life. As in the sexual experience, nothing can exist meaningfully without its opposite: light and dark, good and evil, positive and negative, ebb and flow, and male and female.

Above The union of *yin* and *yang* is symbolized by this couple in the 'hovering butterflies' position, one of thirty 'heaven and earth' positions, porcelain, Ch'ing Dynasty, China, mid 18th century.

Opposite Jade seal in the form of a phallus decorated with the 'dragon among clouds' design, Ch'ing Dynasty, China, 18th century.

Kundalini

The serpent, associated with evil practices in many cultures, undergoes a transformation in traditional Hindu belief as Kundalini, the agent of awakening, of full spiritual and physical satisfaction. Kundalini lies coiled at the level of the first *chakra* but once awoken by the appropriate techniques of meditation, she rises first to the second *chakra*, the site of the sexual organs, then upwards towards the seventh, and most important, *sahasrara chakra* at the top of the head. It is believed that one obtains pure consciousness when one's energy reaches the seventh chakra.

Opposite Psychic centres represented in gilded relief, southern India, 18th century.

Below The *chakras* as flower-heads: the petals symbolize vibration frequencies.

Secret harmonies

The Tantric follower seeking knowledge of cosmic harmony and of the elimination of the male-female antagonism, may intone a mantra, using syllables based on vibrations symbolizing the stages of Kundalini awakening the *chakras*. In Tantric Buddhism the *yab-yum* ('father-mother' in Tibetan) represents the sexual union of the male deity with his female consort, depicted as an ecstatic embrace of entangled limbs. The deity is seated in the lotus position and often holds in one hand the *dorje*, a small weapon symbolizing firmness and masculinity, and in the other hand the bell, which represents the female aspect of the pairing.

Opposite Vajra, the embodiment of supreme wisdom, finds union with female wisdom, after the Kundalini energy has finally brought him to a state which transcends sexual duality, gouache, Tibet, 19th century.

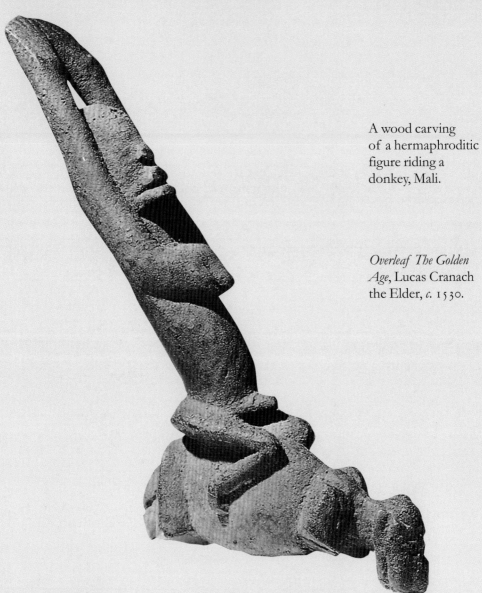

A wood carving
of a hermaphroditic
figure riding a
donkey, Mali.

*Overleaf The Golden
Age*, Lucas Cranach
the Elder, *c.* 1530.

Paradise regained

In the quest for a primeval innocence, when male and female principles were in equilibrium and the serpent had never entered the garden, perhaps the most perfect sexual symbol of all for such harmony is the androgyne, the hermaphrodite. The Greek god Hermaphroditus was the son of the goddess Aphrodite and the god Hermes, and was fused with a female nymph to become a boy with the breasts of a woman.

Other visions of a return to a time of innocence and sexual cosmic equilibrium keep the sexes separate, but not apart, re-affirming a vision of the delicate balance of the primordial sexual forces, as depicted in Lucas Cranach's painting *The Golden Age* (see overleaf).

Below Half-male, half-female deity, sculpture, Bengal, 12th century.

The Tarot

THE TAROT

Its origins shrouded in mystery, the Tarot pack constitutes a body of potent and far-reaching symbolism. The most solid evidence, however, indicates that the Tarot originated in the 15th century in northern Italy as a pack of playing cards. The oldest surviving Tarot cards come from an unnumbered deck painted *c.* 1450 by the artist Bonifacio Bembo for the Visconti-Sforza family of Milan. Games with the cards – sometimes using packs of varying extent – then spread into the rest of Europe, but the first direct description of them did not appear until 1659 in France.

The connection of the Tarot with the occult and divination looks back to a relatively short tradition begun by Antoine Court de Gébelin (1725–84), a Swiss Protestant pastor and Freemason. His beliefs – essentially that the Tarot represented aspects of ancient esoteric mysteries – were taken up by occultists on both sides of the Atlantic towards the end of the 19th century, notoriously by the Order of the Golden Dawn, which counted poets W. B. Yeats and Aleister Crowley among its members.

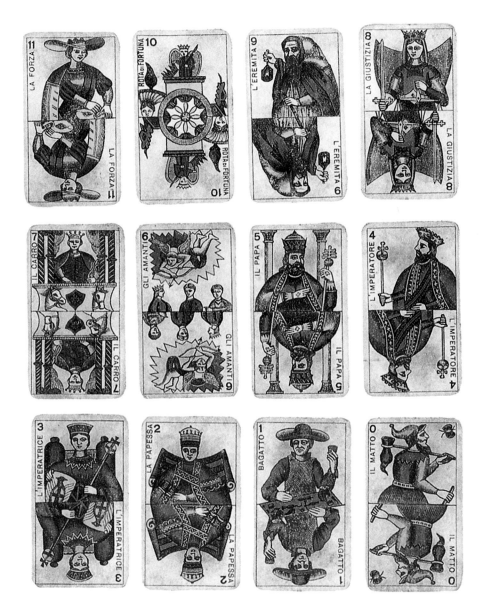

Whatever its origins, the symbolism of the Tarot does lend a richness to the use of the pack for divination. Perhaps, as Jung suggested, man repeats archetypal patterns from his unconscious, even if the cards have no direct descent from ancient wisdoms and mysteries. These patterns embody the real fascination of the Tarot: the counter pointing of good and evil, of the male and female principles, and the interaction of the four elements: air, water, fire and earth.

Modern Tarot packs, of seventy-eight cards, consist of twenty-one numbered trump cards and one unnumbered card (the Fool or Joker), and four suits of ten pip cards and four court cards. Each card may have the possibility of appearing upside-down during a divination reading, in which case the meaning of the card is often thought to be 'reversed', opening up another possible interpretation. Many packs are notable for their graphic brilliance and ingenuity; the illustrations in this book have therefore been drawn from a wide range of designs through the ages as a beautiful introduction to a subject of depth and complexity.

THE MAJOR ARCANA

The strange, esoteric symbolism of the Tarot trump cards exercises a compelling attraction through its vivid yet ambiguous imagery. Here, portrayed through the archetypes of religious and secular experience, are the great issues of life; these are the cards which relate to the underlying principles of existence. Taken as a whole, the sequence, from one to twenty-one, is often compared to a journey from childhood to death, followed by resurrection. In other words, a rite of passage from innocent beginnings to final illumination.

I
The Magician

This figure neatly exemplifies the transition of the Tarot through the centuries from being simply a playing deck to a means of divination. Traditionally, the Magician was shown selling various objects from a table or stall, while bearing a wand indicative of his skill and magical powers. His other hand points to the objects before him to symbolize his ability to control practical affairs. In later versions of the card, a sceptre, cups, a sword and coins (or pentacles) can be seen set before him – the four key elements of practical life, the four suits of the Tarot and a multi-layered opportunity for the fortune-teller.

KEY ASSOCIATIONS
Confident and able in the
direction of everyday life;
persuasive and charming
in communication and
negotiation.

REVERSE ASPECTS
Lack of confidence and
inability to communicate;
inefficient, even cunning
and crafty.

2
The High Priestess

In traditional Tarot packs this card was referred to as the Papess, or female pope; she is associated with the dream world, the realms of the unconscious and with intuitive knowledge. She is often seen seated between pillars, known as Boaz and Jakim, or Alpha and Omega, a reference to the pillars of the Temple of Solomon in Jerusalem; one is coloured black, symbol of the feminine principles of mystery and intuition, while its white counterpart expresses masculine rationalism.

KEY ASSOCIATIONS
True, intuitive wisdom and knowledge; the feminine side of the male personality.

REVERSE ASPECTS
Superficiality; lack of personal harmony; suppression of the feminine or intuitive side of the personality.

3
The Empress

associated with the more practical, motherly aspects of the
female principle, this figure may be represented as a dignified
though kindly, queen-like presence, sometimes surrounded by
symbols of fertility, a reference to child-bearing, marriage and
domesticity. The Empress is practical, kind and generous in her
attitude to others.

KEY ASSOCIATIONS
Steadfastness in action; promotion
of well-being and security.

REVERSE ASPECTS
Lack of action and concentration;
possible domestic problems, even
difficulties in child-bearing.

4
The Emperor

responsibility and firmness are present in every aspect of this omnipotent figure. The sense of power is expressed in his posture: he faces sideways, thus distancing himself from the viewer. His control of the physical world is indicated in his crossed legs, which form the figure '4', symbolizing the four elements.

KEY ASSOCIATIONS
Ability to shoulder
responsibility;
forcefulness in
development and
execution.

REVERSE ASPECTS
Opposition to authority;
immaturity and
indecision.

5
The Hierophant or Pope

a symbol of religious authority in
the traditional Tarot pack, this figure
is now more likely to be associated
with the idea of informed professional
advice or counselling. The Hierophant
– a priest of the sacred mysteries of
Greece – may be accompanied by
two other figures in the foreground
of the card, who are seekers of
knowledge and benediction.
Sometimes these are represented
simply by hands reaching up to
touch the vestments of the holy man.

KEY ASSOCIATIONS
Religious guidance and authority; constructive counsel.

REVERSE ASPECTS
Dubious advice; misleading and inappropriate comment.

KEY ASSOCIATIONS
Making difficult decisions, not necessarily about love; considering important commitments.

REVERSE ASPECTS
Postponing choices; being indecisive or making bad decisions.

6
The Lovers

This card has been subject to a number of representations and interpretations through the ages. The traditional form, of which there were a number of variants, showed a man choosing between two women, while a corpulent Cupid directed his arrow at the suitor's heart. Later versions of the card show Adam and Eve in the Garden of Eden, although these tend to obscure the card's main associations with choice and making the right decision.

7
The Chariot

the chariot in question is drawn by two horses without reins
(in some versions they may be replaced by sphinxes). The
charioteer, crowned and wearing armour, is thus seen to be
directing the horses by sheer willpower, hence the association
of the card with the human ego and ambition. Some cards show
one black and one white horse – the female and male principles –
indicating that the various conflicting aspects of personality
have been brought under control by strength of character.

KEY ASSOCIATIONS
Ability to overcome adverse
situations; ambition and
decisiveness in achieving
one's ends.

REVERSE ASPECTS
Loss of control; chaos in one's
personal life and disregard
for others.

8
Justice

One of three of the four cardinal virtues to be represented in the Tarot pack – the others are Fortitude and Temperance – Justice has been subject to shifting representations. In some packs, for instance, she appeared as card 11, while card 11, Strength, was switched to 8, to coincide with the order of the Zodiac and their respective associations with Libra and Leo. Justice is represented as a woman – as are all the virtue cards – seated in a posture of judgment and holding the traditional sword and scales, which represent accountability and balance.

KEY ASSOCIATIONS
Fair and reasonable judgment; triumph over bigotry and prejudice.

REVERSE ASPECTS
Unfair or delayed judgment; inequality and bias.

9
The Hermit

the traditional representation of this figure is as an old man wearing a long habit and carrying a lantern; this is sometimes replaced by an hourglass, suggesting a connection with time and patience. Since a hermit is one who has isolated himself from other human beings, he may be seen to symbolize independence and introspection, and a need for soul-searching. If this card appears during a reading it will probably indicate a need for reflective, individual decision-making.

KEY ASSOCIATIONS
Need for prudence; need
to reach into one's inner
resources.

REVERSE ASPECTS
Isolation from others; a
negative resistance to
help.

10
The Wheel of Fortune

the central motif of this card is the wheel itself to which a number of animals cling precariously. Above the wheel is a presiding figure, which may sometimes take the form of the goddess Fortuna or that of a sphinx. The dominant theme of this card is clearly the role which random events play in our lives in the form, hopefully, of good fortune and unexpected luck. A reversed card, though, can indicate the exact opposite – chance misfortune, which may strike in spite of all our efforts to achieve a favourable set of circumstances.

KEY ASSOCIATIONS
Unexpected good
fortune; success
without striving.

REVERSE ASPECTS
Failure in spite of all
efforts; unexpected
bad luck.

II
Strength

One of the virtue cards in the Tarot pack, Strength may be personified by a woman holding open the jaws of a lion, or by Hercules in combat with the Nemean lion. In a positive sense, the lion can represent inner strength and courage, as long as the powerful emotions in play have been properly channelled and controlled. A reversed card here has negative implications, indicating an inability to exercise self-control.

KEY ASSOCIATIONS
Strength and power under
control; the virtue of
fortitude.

REVERSE ASPECTS
Feelings of inadequacy
and powerlessness; power
wrongly used.

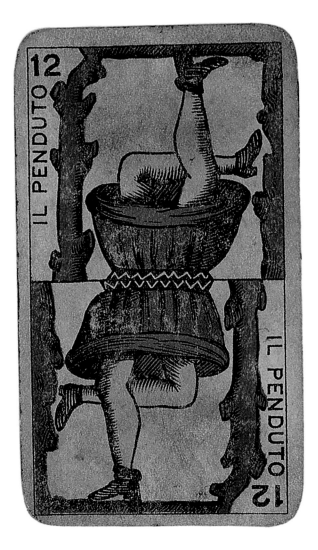

KEY ASSOCIATIONS
Devotion to worthwhile
ends; sacrifice in pursuit
of a greater good.

REVERSE ASPECTS
Lack of commitment;
apathy in pursuit of goals.

12
The Hanged Man

this is one of the most mysterious cards in the pack and one which has defied most attempts at a satisfactory explanation of its significance. The central figure hangs by one leg from a crosspiece, but is usually portrayed with a contented expression on his face. Some versions show coins falling from his pockets, as though to indicate that he is giving up worldly and material wealth, thus associating the card with the concept of sacrifice.

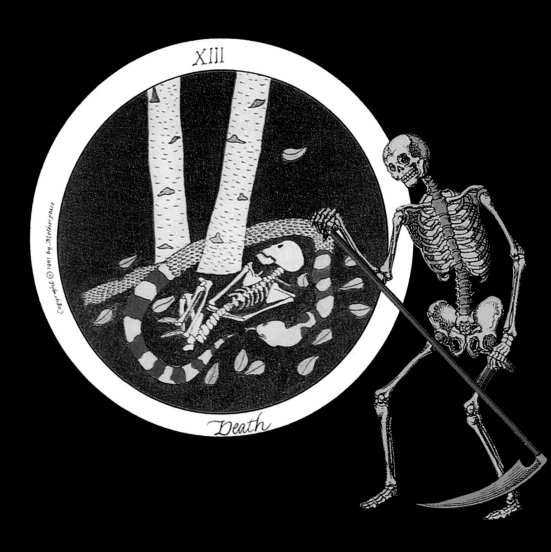

XIII

Death

Copyright © 1981 by Mediarspace

13
Death

In most versions this card displays a personification of death in the form of a skeleton wielding a scythe, surrounded by the severed limbs of recent victims. But in spite of its gruesome aspect, Death is rarely an indication of actual death, but rather of the change from one phase of life to another. This can even be a happy occurrence, such as the beginning of a new relationship, although there is a strong implication that the change must be accepted with a positive attitude.

KEY ASSOCIATIONS
Change and alteration; the beginning of a new life.

REVERSE ASPECTS
Unpleasant, painful change; slow and possibly agonizing periods of transition.

14
Temperance

the virtue card Temperance depicts a woman. In most cases she is a winged figure seen pouring some liquid from one flask to another; the prominence of the wings on the figure's back has led some commentators to speculate that her origins are angelic, although it is more likely that she is derived from winged female figures of Classical antiquity. The passage of the liquid from one container to another indicates the need to find the right blend in all things, to mix various elements until the correct balance is found.

KEY ASSOCIATIONS
Balance, especially in matters of personality; maturity in handling difficult circumstances.

REVERSE ASPECTS
Conflicting interests; fickleness in making decisions.

15
The Devil

the most common image on this card is the depiction of the central figure of the Devil, sometimes winged and sometimes in the form of a goat, below which are two other demonic figures apparently leashed around the neck. Another variation shows the Devil as a horned god, perhaps derived from the Celtic stag god Cernunnos, who had associations with fertility. Like Death, the meaning of this card is not direct; rather than symbolizing all things truly demonic, its main connotation is of inconvenience, of the unpleasant details, which are an ineluctable part of life.

KEY ASSOCIATIONS
Feeling of frustration and oppression; overbearing weight of the material side of life.

REVERSE ASPECTS
More exaggerated forms of the above; true evil.

THE DEVIL.

KEY ASSOCIATIONS
Disturbance and ruin;
sudden, violent loss.

REVERSE ASPECTS
Less severe forms
of the above.

16
The Lightning-struck Tower

THE TOWER OF DESTRUCTION

although this card seems to indicate total disaster at first sight, as with most of the more alarming cards in the Tarot pack, there is a somewhat brighter side. The immediate image, though, is disturbing enough: a crowned tower is struck by a thunderbolt, causing the occupants to be hurled through the window to their deaths. The crown is shown to be dislodged by the jolt, which may indicate a blow to the personal ego. But while the card does undoubtedly signify something very disturbing and possibly violent, there may sometimes be the implication that something useful can be learned from the experience. Reversed, the card may indicate a less severe form of experience than in its upright position.

17
The Star

the dominant figure of the card is a naked woman pouring water
from two flagons on to the ground. Some commentators have
identified her as the Babylonian goddess Ishtar who sought the
waters of life to revivify her dead lover. In the sky behind the
figure is a very large star surrounded by seven smaller ones,
possibly the Pleiades. The theme of restoration to health and life is
dominant here, especially after a period of tribulation and stress.

KEY ASSOCIATIONS
Renewal and fresh hope;
promise of fulfilment.

REVERSE ASPECTS
Diminished life; some
obstacles to happiness,
but it can still be achieved.

18
The Moon

this is a very negative card: an old woman's face fills the moon at the head of the card – another aspect of the feminine principle, but now implying age and loneliness. A dog and wolf howl at the moon while, from the pool in the foreground of the image, a sinister-looking crayfish crawls, like a vision from the murkier depths of the spirit. There is a strong sense of lack of direction and confusion, of being caught in a web of personal error.

KEY ASSOCIATIONS
Personal depression; confusion arising from an inability to see things clearly.

REVERSE ASPECTS
Exaggerated forms of the above; despair and a desperate need for help.

19
The Sun

One of the most optimistic images in the Tarot pack, the sun signifies high ideals of achievement and feelings of balance and happiness. The traditional representation of the sun itself is with a human face, which beams down benevolently on twin children apparently standing in a walled garden. Sometimes a child may be shown mounted on a horse, an animal traditionally associated with Jupiter and therefore a potent solar symbol.

KEY ASSOCIATIONS
Happiness and contentment in achieving success.

REVERSE ASPECTS
Diminished forms of the above.

20
The Last Judgment

Since this card refers to the day of reckoning, its implications are of looking back, of taking stock of things that have happened. The dead are shown in the foreground of the card, rising from their graves, summoned by the blast on the trumpet of the angel who dominates the upper part of the card. The antithesis between the upright position and its reverse is clear-cut. In the first instance, there is cause for a satisfaction with a phase of life just completed; in the second, there may very well be remorse or regret.

KEY ASSOCIATIONS
Satisfactory outcome of a period of life or a specific matter.

REVERSE ASPECTS
Regret over recent events; possible delay in concluding a sequence of actions.

21
The Universe

This card is one of the best demonstrations in the whole pack of just how rich Tarot symbolism is. A naked woman dances within the form of a laurel wreath, while the corners of the card harbour the four creatures of the prophet Ezekiel's vision, which may evoke the four elements of matter and the four fixed signs of the Zodiac (Aquarius, Leo, Scorpio and Taurus). A Christian reading of the Tarot could take them to represent the four evangelists. This is an especially positive card, indicating the successful completion of a phase of life and the promising start to the next.

KEY ASSOCIATIONS
Successful completion; a sense of repleteness.

REVERSE ASPECTS
Frustrations; inability to bring something to a satis-factory end.

THE MINOR

Two types of card make up the four suits of the Minor Arcana: the court cards which, unlike the conventional playing-card deck, include a Knight, and the pip cards, so-called because only the suit symbols, or 'pips', were traditionally illustrated. The Aces, however, do stand somewhat apart since, in their singularity, they represent the very essence of their respective suits, each one of which is highly individual.

ARCANA

For instance, Sceptres and Swords are considered male suits, while Cups and Pentacles/Coins are associated with the female principle. Fire is the element of Sceptres, water of Cups, air of Swords, and earth of Pentacles/Coins. In general, too, the significance of the Minor Arcana has much more to do with our everyday lives, in contrast to the Major Arcana cards, which represent the great underlying principles of the universe.

Sceptres King

KING of WANDS

The embodiment of responsibility and positive thinking, this King is often associated with a paternal role. He is enterprising and caring in his upright position – considerate to others and fair in judgment. The strength of his personality, however, may only too easily turn to intolerance and, reversed, he can indicate an inability to appreciate other peoples' points of view, especially if he believes their moral standards are lower than his.

Sceptres Queen

One of the most prominent occultists of the 19th century, S. L. MacGregor Mathers, associated this Queen with a woman living in the country, a lady of the manor. Like the King she is capable, but honest and fair in her dealings with other people. Indeed, the court cards are very much concerned with personal qualities and the Sceptres often express human action in achieving something rather than the significance of what is achieved. Reversed, the Queen's essential good nature may give way to a wish to dominate or even to bitterness.

THE QUEEN OF CLUBS

Sceptres Knight

Of all the court cards, the Knights are very much an expression of movement and energy. In the case of the Knight of Sceptres, there is a suspicion that his actions, though well-meant, may remain uncompleted – a quality symbolized by the gap between the mouths and tails of the salamanders which decorate his doublet. There is, though, a negative side to the Knight, especially when reversed, in which his own enthusiasm and fiery quality are at odds with people around him, leading to discord and breakdown in relations.

Sceptres Knave

Sometimes referred to as Pages, the Knaves represent the dominant quality of each suit in a more light-hearted way than their seniors in the pack. Thus, the positive and outgoing aspects of Sceptres take on the form of youthful enthusiasm, of the desire to bring light and excitement to people around. Of course, such an engaging set of characteristics can have its negative side. If circumstances are not propitious, then the Knave's simple, honest qualities can turn to petulance and weakness – a bearer of bad news.

VALET DE BÂTON

Sceptres Ten to Six

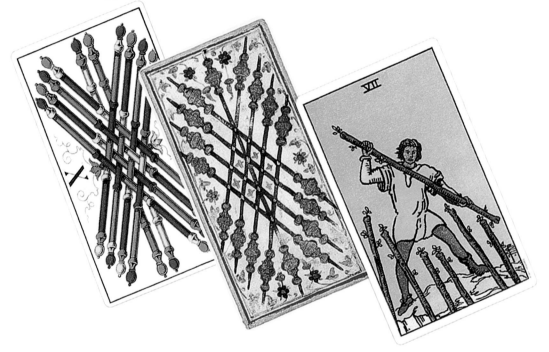

	KEY ASSOCIATIONS	REVERSE ASPECTS
TEN	Honourable conduct	Treachery
NINE	Discipline and order	Disarray and delay
EIGHT	Harmony and understanding	Disagreement and dispute
SEVEN	Successful advance	Retreat and indecision
SIX	Hopefulness	Indecision

Sceptres Five to Deuce

	KEY ASSOCIATIONS	REVERSE ASPECTS
FIVE	Material good fortune	Hurt and ruin
FOUR	Four-square strength	Unorthodox happiness and prosperity
THREE	Commercial enterprise	Reflection and stock-taking
TWO	Success in material things	Change, entering the unknown

Sceptres Ace

the singularity of the Aces implies a unique concentration of the major associations of the suit – in this case, fire. Here is strength, power, creative inspiration and vast sexual energy, all expressed in the fecundity of the branch-like sceptre. This card is a veritable burst of energy and hope. But the sheer assertiveness of the card also means that the reverse is correspondingly catastrophic: chaos and ruin, perhaps because the great commitment and creativity of the Sceptres have been misdirected.

Cups King

The Cups are associated with water, a gentler, more soulful element than the fire of the Sceptres. This is the force of the inner life and consequently, the King of Cups is a thinking person, perhaps a lawyer or doctor. That he is powerful is beyond doubt; we have only to note the way in which he grasps his cup, as though it were part of his regalia. Yet, he is quite a cool character and may be suspected of having a troubled inner life. Reversed, his undoubted creativity may involve him in dishonesty or corruption.

ROI DE COUPE

Cups Queen

This is an especially 'happy' card, indicating balance and harmony. The cup on this card is always the most elaborate in the suit, as though to symbolize the high achievements made possible by the responsible use of the imagination. The Queen regards it almost lovingly, showing her concern that the forces symbolized should be directed towards worthy ends. Kindly, understanding, sometimes mysterious, she is undoubtedly an agent for good. Her spirituality, however, can appear as instability and fickleness if the card is reversed.

Cups Knight

again, like the King and Queen, the Knight expresses the power of the creative forces of life, but he is less focused and less powerful than the two senior figures. Though well-meaning, he may sometimes give way to fantasy rather than use his imagination to get at the deeper truths of life. Indeed, there is often an ambivalence in his way of gazing at his cup, as though he is slightly uncertain of his true nature. His presence may herald change and new excitements, especially of a romantic nature but, reversed, there is unreliability and recklessness.

Prince of Cups

Cups Knave

the most innocent of the Cup court cards, the knave has yet to suffer the inner conflicts of his seniors. His gentle gaze falls uncomplicatedly upon his cup, shown in certain packs to contain a fish, symbol of imagination. Studiously confident, the Knave may represent undeveloped talents; his presence may indicate that a time for quiet reflection has arrived. The reverse position of this thoughtful young man is one of laziness, of neglect of skills, of failure to make meaningful commitments, of shallow self-indulgence.

Cups Ten to Six

	KEY ASSOCIATIONS	REVERSE ASPECTS
TEN	Good reputation and honour	Strife and dispute
NINE	Overcoming difficulty	Falling into error
EIGHT	Security and attachment	Fantasy and risk
SEVEN	Imaginative power	Delusion and indecision
SIX	Sense of the past	Exaggerated nostalgia

Cups Five to Deuce

	KEY ASSOCIATIONS	REVERSE ASPECTS
FIVE	Espousal and union	False starts
FOUR	Apathy, dwelling on past experience	Awakening to the new
THREE	Wonder and joy	Loss of happiness
TWO	Affection, love	Breakdown, ending

Cups Ace

an intense card, this Ace is
the essence of love and all
the positive powers of the
unconscious mind. It bears, in
various forms, the image of a
great and elaborate cup, which
can be identified with the Holy
Grail, the repository of the Holy
Spirit and the unifying force of
the world. It was, however, the
departure of the Grail from the
land of King Arthur, which
brought about the downfall
and disintegration of Camelot.
Similarly, this card reversed is a
symbol of disruption, of times
changing for the worse.

Swords King

KING OF SWORDS

© 1970 U.S. Games

The suit of Swords is most directly associated with the element of air and therefore with matters of the spirit. But the sword is clearly a dangerous weapon and may cause pain and wounding but, by the same token, it can be used to cut through deception and subterfuge to arrive at a final truth. This King is a ruler indeed, a law-maker, a man of independent judgment, an achiever in whatever he does. The implications of a reversed card are alarming: probability of great disruption, abuse of power and contempt for the weak.

Swords Queen

a courageous woman, the Queen may very well have suffered deep sorrow and loss. Somehow, however, with the aid of her sword, she has managed to overcome setbacks, achieving a sense of truth and inner wisdom. The sword is held erect, symbol of her moral rectitude; it also stands for the ability of women in general to come through suffering, especially at the hands of men, to a state of grace. We must beware, though, of the Queen reversed, of sorrow for sorrow's sake, of malice and wrongdoing in response to adverse circumstances.

Kali

Reine des Epées   Regina di Spade
Queen of Swords
Königin der Schwerter   Reina de Espadas

Swords Knight

KNIGHT of SWORDS .

Significantly, the Knight's sword is held at an angle or even brandished in the air. We may understand that although he is brave and skilful – he may even be a professional soldier – the Knight has a wild side to his character. This is greatly exaggerated when the card is reversed: bravery becomes impetuousness, skill at arms becomes the unnecessary use of force, application of great energy becomes simple-minded indulgence.

Swords Knave

a card often associated with spying, of surveying the activity of other people, but from a detached point of view, the Knave raises himself above immediate conflict. Detachment is a very important quality for this figure, but if he does get more closely involved in any situation, then he will weigh up the pros and cons very carefully. There is, however, a side to the Knave, which speaks of an inability to deal directly with a problem or to act positively in adverse circumstances – the fatal flaw of Shakespeare's Hamlet.

THE KNAVE OF SWORDS

Swords Ten to Six

	KEY ASSOCIATIONS	REVERSE ASPECTS
TEN	Misfortune and sorrow	Temporary good fortune
NINE	Tranquil conscience, good behaviour	Suspicion and distrust
EIGHT	Oppression, illness	Change, accident, liberation
SEVEN	Impulse, sudden desire	Specific advice, counsel
SIX	Gradual change, travelling	Unexpected developments

Swords Five to Deuce

	KEY ASSOCIATIONS	REVERSE ASPECTS
FIVE	Loss and defeat	Accentuation of these
FOUR	Withdrawal, retreat	Return
THREE	Extreme pain and sorrow	Mental and spiritual confusion
TWO	Precarious balance in adversity, courage	Violence and treachery

Swords Ace

the Swords suit is very much a masculine one, associated with the ability to act rationally, but also with loss, pain and destruction. In its purest form, then, the Ace is the symbol of strongly constituted authority, of the ability to pursue a line of enquiry to an ultimate truth. If this clarity is no longer there – when the card is reversed – then confusion and exaggeration in thought, feeling and deed will ensue.

Pentacles King

the courtly figures of the Pentacles suit are much more down-to-earth than those of the rest of the Tarot pack. This underlines the nature of Pentacles as the magical sign for the world around us – a more actual presence than air, fire and water. In some packs this is the suit of Coins, indicating an even more limited focus on the material world. Appropriately, then, the King looks more like a successful merchant than a regal figure. He is a capable man in his professional life, but still enjoys the comforts and delights of home and garden. His reversal implies failure and weakness.

THE KING OF MONEY

Pentacles Queen

QUEEN of PENTACLES

The Queen's closeness to the pulse of life is often evident in the intensity of the gaze she directs towards her pentacle. Sometimes this impression is reinforced by presenting her seated amid symbols of fecundity – a burgeoning garden, with roses and a rabbit. The patroness of Pentacles is the Empress, a passionate yet practical trump card, and the Queen undoubtedly derives certain characteristics from this association – notably a generosity of soul, but tempered by a greater consciousness of the practical world. On the negative side, she may be pursued by self-doubt and distrust.

Pentacles Knight

a less adventurous fellow than the other Knights of the Tarot, the Knight of Pentacles displays an engaging simplicity and trustworthiness in his attitude to life. His existence may be rather uneventful, but he is dependable and will generally achieve his objectives in the fullness of time. Even the posture and bulk of his horse seem to suggest that this Knight has very little fantasy or romance in his life. This lack of adventure, of dash and bravura, becomes much more exaggerated if the card is reversed; what was practical common sense becomes simply dullness.

Pentacles Knave

This youthful figure – possibly a student, but in any case someone setting out in life – is usually shown in close contemplation of his pentacle. It is as though he is completely caught up in his chosen discipline, to the exclusion of all outside matters. The dedication to his task and the seriousness which he brings to his work do make the Knave a very negative personage if the card is reversed. The careful, responsible approach is transformed into slow-wittedness and bumbling.

Pentacles Ten to Six

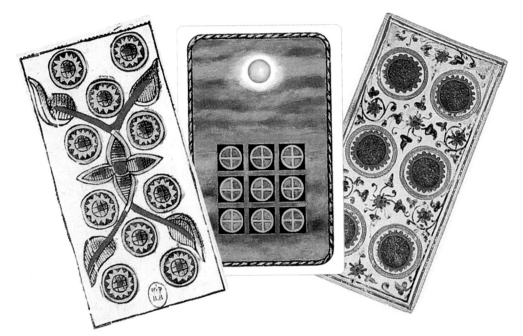

	KEY ASSOCIATIONS	REVERSE ASPECTS
TEN	The hearth, family solidarity	Recklessness and loss
NINE	Patience, care	Deception, unsound practice
EIGHT	Attractiveness with modesty	Superficiality, hypocrisy
SEVEN	Venality, materialism	Financial worry
SIX	Offerings, satisfaction	Unreasonable, overweening ambition

Pentacles Five to Deuce

KEY ASSOCIATIONS	REVERSE ASPECTS
FIVE	Partnership, unspoilt love	Lechery and licentiousness
FOUR	Unalloyed pleasure	Objection and prevention
THREE	High rank and public service	Beginnings, unrewarding work
TWO	Precarious balance, arranged pleasure	Irresponsibility, forced jollity

Pentacles Ace

If the suit of Pentacles as a whole represents the varieties of well-being in the world around us, then the Ace is the quintessence of such feelings of contentment and happiness. Upright, the card has the positive connotations of enjoyment of everyday things, of a celebration of the bounty of nature, encapsulated especially in the form of the garden. Yet such wealth and plenty can also be seen as corrupting, as encouraging selfishness and over-indulgence in material comfort.

Illustration and text credits

The following abbreviations have been used: a above, b below, bg background, c centre, l left, r right.

Title Pages

(from left to right)
Cairo Museum. British Museum London. Photo
© British Museum, London. Copyright Merle
Greene Robertson, 1976. The Victoria & Albert
Museum, London (Photo Eileen Tweedy). Photo
Wellcome Institute Library, London. © Christina
Gascoigne. Private collection. Ajit Mookerjee
Collection. With kind authorization of Frances
Cartes BP 49–45130 Sain Max– France.

Ancient Egypt

The Walters Art Gallery, Baltimore 64. Staatliche
Museen Berlin, Bildarchiv Preussischer Kulturbesitz
32. Brooklyn Museum (49.48 Charles Edwin Wilbour
Fund) 72. Cairo Museum 3, 14, 46, 76–77; (photo
Gallimard, l'Univers des Formes, Paris) 57, 78; (photo
Kodansha Ltd, Tokyo) 50; (photo Albert Shoucair)
36, 68, 69, 70, 74. Photo Peter Clayton 87. Ny
Carlsberg Glyptotek, Copenhagen 52. Photo André
Held 56. Roemer-und Pelizaeus-Museum,
Hildesheim 83. Photo Max Hirmer 35. Photo
Kodansha Ltd, Tokyo 55, 59, 82. British Museum,
London 15, 24–25, 27, 28, 29, 31, 33, 37, 44, 45, 63,
65, 66, 72, 75, 89. Photo Kazimierz Michalowski
16–17, 42. Musée du Louvre, Paris, © Photo RMN 60.
Photo James Putnam 80–81. Photo John Ross 48–49.
Photo Scala 39. Photo Chris Scarre 84.

Quotations from *The Ancient Egyptian Book of the Dead*
are taken from the translation by Raymond O.
Faulkner, revised edition, published by British
Museum Press.

The Celts

Photo Aerofilms 101. National Museum, Budapest
130. Musée de Chatillon-sur-Seine (photo Jean
Roubier) 115. Nationalmuseet, Copenhagen 127, 139,
146, 147, 157. National Museum of Ireland, Dublin
145, 161, 162. Courtesy Board of Trinity College
Dublin 133, 158–159, 165, 166, 167. Photo Werner
Forman Archive 98. British Museum, London 135,
150, 152, 154, 156. Musée Borély, Marseilles 108–109.
Photo George Mott 102. Prähistorische
Staatssammlung, Munich 134. Museum of
Antiquities, Newcastle 105. Bibliothèque Nationale
de France, Paris 121; (Cabinet des Médailles) 111*a*,
140. National Museum, Prague 118. Landesmuseum
für Vor-und Frühgeschichte, Saarbrücken 124,
142–143. Musée des Antiquités Nationales, St-
Germain-en-Laye (photo © RMN) 90, 112.
Historisches Museum der Pfalz, Speyer 136.
Württembergisches Landesmuseum, Stuttgart 122.
Photo Homer Sykes 96–97. Photo Telegraph Colour
Library 128–129. Naturhistorisches Museum, Vienna
131. All drawings, unless detailed above, are
reproduced by kind permission of Aidan Meehan
(© Aidan Meehan).

The Native Americans

Courtesy the Anschutz Collection 179. Tony
Campbell 227. E. C. Curtis 170, 205. Werner
Forman Archive 174, 190, 191, 200, 216, 219, 224,
228, 233, 237; (Alaska Gallery of Eskimo Art) 234;
(Maxwell Museum of Anthropology, Albuquerque)
184; (Anchorage Museum of History and Art) 232;
(Ethnologisches Museum, Berlin) 193, 240; (Field
Museum of Natural History, Chicago) 177; (Plains
Indians Museum, Buffalo Bill Historical Center,
Cody, Wyoming) 168, 172, 176; (British Museum,

London) 199; (National Museum of the American Indian, Smithsonian Institution, New York) 189, 206, 210, 213; (Private Collection, New York) 241; (National Museum of Man, Ottawa, Ontario) 214, 231, 236; (University of Pennsylvania Museum, Philadelphia) 203; (Haffenreffer Museum of Anthropology, Brown University, Providence) 182; (Arizona State Museum, Tucson) 79; (University of British Columbia, Vancouver) 238; (Provincial Museum, Victoria, British Columbia) 198, 209, 230, 235. Copyright British Museum, London 244. National Museum of the American Indian, Smithsonian Institution, New York 186. Franc J. Newcomb *Sandpaintings of the Navajo Shooting Chant*, 1938, 204–205. Sally Nicholls 222–223. Private collection 197. The Wheelwright Museum of the American Indian, Santa Fe 179, 221, 242. Museum für Volkerkunde, Vienna 194. Eva Wilson *North American Indian Designs*, 1984, 168, 175, 178, 201, 202, 207, 211, 212, 229.

The Maya

The Baltimore Museum of Art, Gift of Alan Wurtzburger 314. Drawing by C. P. Beetz, after originals by J. A. Fox 305. Museum of Fine Arts, Boston, Gift of Landon T. Clay 247, 263, 278. Copyright British Museum 286, 297. Drawing by Michael Coe 271*l*, 290–291. T. Patrick Culbert *Maya Civilization*, 1993, 249. Dallas Museum of Art, The Eugene and Margaret McDermott Fund in honor of Mrs Alex Spence 322. Copyright © 1985 Founders Society Detroit Institute of Arts, Founders Society purchase, Katherine Margaret Kay Bequest Fund and New Endowment Fund 308*l*. Duke University Museum of Art, Durham, Museum Purchase 280–81. From a copy by Felipe Dávalos, courtesy of the Florida State Museum, Gainesville 246. J. G. Fuller/The Hutchinson Library, UK 306. Museo Popol Vuh, Universidad Francisco Marroquín, Guatemala City 289. F. H. A. von Humboldt *Nouvelle Espagne Atlas*, 1810, 255, 273. Photo © Justin Kerr 247, 257, 261, 263, 265, 266, 270, 278, 280–81, 283, 284, 289, 293, 294, 295, 309, 314, 320–321, 323. Viscount Edward Kingsborough *Antiquities of Mexico Volume III*, 1830, 276. Finn Lewis/The Hutchinson Library, UK: 251. A. P. Maudslay *Biologia Centrali Americana Volume II*, 1889–1902, 296. Instituto de Cultura de Tabasco, Dirección de Patrimonio Cultural, Museo Regional de Antropologia "Carlos Pellicer Cámara", Villahermosa 268. Museo Nacional de Antropologia, Mexico 299, 301. Drawing by Mary Miller 308*r*. New Orleans Museum of Art, Ella West Freeman Foundation Matching Fund 293; Women's Volunteer Committee Fund 295. American Museum of Natural History, New York 307. J. Pate/The Hutchinson Library, UK 313. Courtesy Peabody Museum, Harvard University, Cambridge 302–303, 310–311, 317. Edwin Pearlman, M.D., Norfolk, Virginia 270. Drawing by Diane Griffiths Peck 275. Princeton University Art Museum, Gift of the Hans and Dorothy Widenmann Foundation 323. Private collection 257, 265, 266. Copyright Merle Greene Robertson, 1976, 258, 304. Saint Louis Art Museum, Gift of Morton D. May 320–321. Drawing by Linda Schele 259, 267, 271*r*, 277, 280*a*, 288, 289, 292, 300, 316*r*. Paul Schellhas *Representation of Deities of Mayan Manuscripts*, 1904, 298. Robert J. Sharer *The Ancient Maya*, 1994, 282. Drawing by Karl Taube 252, 260, 262, 264, 285, 315. Antonio Tejeda 310–311. After J. E. S. Thompson *The Rise and Fall of Maya Civilization*, 1956, 253. Wilson G. Turner *Maya Designs*, 1980, 318. Utah Museum of Fine Arts, Salt Lake City, Permanent Collection 284.

The Buddha

Martin Brauen 368. Indian Museum, Calcutta 334. University Library, Cambridge 392–93. Ananda K. Coomaraswamy, *Elements of Buddhist Iconography*, 1935, 328, 333, 337, 348, 377. After A. van Gabain, *Das Uigurische Königreich*, 1960, 401. Bernard P. Groslier *Hinterindien*, 1962, 391. Graham Harrison 326, 354, 374, 382, 398–99, 402. Martin Hürlimann 370, 390. The Nelson-Atkins Museum of Art (Nelson Fund), Kansas City 373. Kozan-ji, Kyoto 380. Toji, Kyoto 379. By permission of the British Library, London 327, 342–43, 371, 389. Copyright British Museum, London 336, 340, 345, 353, 356–57, 358, 364, 367, 372, 375, 388, 400. By courtesy of the Board of Trustees of the Victoria & Albert Museum, London 329, 351, 359. Los Angeles County Museum of Art, Mr and Mrs Harry Lenart 350. Lu K'uan Yü *Taoist Yoga*, 1970, 403. John Lundquist 385. Staatliches Museum für Völkerkunde, Munich 332, 347, 376. Collection of the Newark Museum, Newark, Gift of Herman and Paul Jaehne, 1941 (Photo John Bigelow Taylor) 349; Purchase 1920, Shelton Collection (Photo John Bigelow Taylor) 395. Musée Guimet, Paris 363, 386; (Giraudon) 339; (© PHOTO R.M.N.) 335, 338. The State Hermitage, St Petersburg (Photo John Bigelow Taylor) 326; Prince Ukhtomsky Collection (Photo John Bigelow Taylor) 361. Asian Art Museum of San Francisco, The Avery Brundage Collection (Photo John Bigelow Taylor) 344. Archaeological Museum, Sarnath (Photo Martin Hürlimann) 300. Seattle Art Museum 331. *Taisho-shinshu-daizokyo* 384, 394. Toyo Bunko Library, Tokyo 381, 397. Smithsonian Institution, Washington D.C. 396.

The Tao

Bowes Museum, Barnard Castle, Durham 453r. Palace Museum, Beijing 442, 476–7. The Oriental Museum, Durham University 409, 414, 418, 422, 423, 429bg, 438l, 439, 443, 446, 449, 450, 451, 461. Feng Yun-p'eng & Feng Yun-yuan, *Chin Shih So*, 1906, 117, 437br. After J. J. M. de Groot *The Religious System of China*, 1892–1910, 408. *Hui Ming Ching* 467. The Nelson-Atkins Museum of Art (Nelson Fund), Kansas City 436. John Lagerwey, member of the École française d'Extrême-Orient (EFEO) 415, 416, 426a, 459. Lin Ling-su, *Tao-tsang*, early 12th century, 405. Copyright British Museum, London, 407, 420, 453l, 470. Percival David Foundation of Chinese Art, School of Oriental and African Studies, University of London 456. The Hutchinson Library, London, © Melanie Friend 472. Spink & Son Ltd, London 404, 410–11, 430, 434–5, 454. By Courtesy of the Board of Trustees of the Victoria & Albert Museum, London 413, 432, 448, 478–9. Wellcome Institute Library, London 425. New York Public Library, Spencer Collection, Astor, Lennon and Tilden Foundation 445. © Photo Bibliothèque Nationale de France, Paris 419. Private collection 463, 468. R. C. Rudolph and Wen Yu *Han Tomb Art of West China*, 1951, 452. *San-tsai-t'u-hui, c.* 1609, 433. Museum of Art and History, Shanghai 474l. Shojuraigo Temple, Shiga 438b. *Shu Ching T'u Shuo* 428. National Palace Museum, Taipei 440, 460, 462, 471. *Tao-tsang* 426b, 441, 444, 464a, 466, 469. C. Trever *Excavations in Northern Mongolia (1924–5)*, 1932, 455a. Christopher Ward 464b. Yu Yen *Chou I Tshan Thung Chhi Fa Hui*, 1284, 429.

Christianity

Text by James Bentley.
Musées Royaux des Beaux-Arts, Antwerp 6.
Barbier de Montault *Iconographie Chrétienne*,
1890, 530. W. E. C. Baynes *St. Joseph of Arimathaea*,
1929, 548. Rheinisches Landesmuseum, Bonn
524. Museo Civico, Sansepolcro 536. Musée
d'Unterlinden, Colmar 498, 515. Kölnisches
Stadtsmuseum, Cologne 510. Nationalmuseet,
Copenhagen 508. Office of Public Works in
Ireland, Dublin 509. Galleria dell'Accademia,
Florence 488. St Marien Cathedral, Havelberg 514.
Hirmer Fotoarchiv 513, 516. Museo de Escultura,
Lérida 483. By permission of The British Library,
London 485, 491, 500, 506, 507, 544, 554, 555.
Copyright British Museum, London 481, 551.
Reproduced by courtesy of the Trustees, The
National Gallery, London 495, 517, 518, 521,
527, 531, 532, 535, 553. By courtesy of the Board
of Trustees of the Victoria & Albert Museum,
London 545, 552. Santa Maria, Loretto Aprutino
541. Biblioteca Nacional, Madrid 504. Museo
Nacional de Antropologia, Mexico City 519.
Bayerische Staatsbibliothek, Munich 511.
Copyright The Frick Collection, New York 496.
Germanisches Nationalmuseum, Nuremberg 499.
© Photo Bibliothèque Nationale de France, Paris
492, 501, 512, 525, 556–57. Musée National du
Moyen-Age, Thermes de Cluny, Paris 537.
Private collection 549. Museum of Art,
Rhode Island School of Design, Providence
523. Museo delle Terme, Rome 484. Photo Scala
486–87, 488, 498, 515, 522, 533, 536, 541. Schoeffer
Hortus Sanitatis, 1485, 490. Senlis Cathedral 534.
Torcello Cathedral 542. San Pietro, Vatican City 533.
Vatican Museums 493, 494, 502–3, 522, 538.
San Marco, Venice 480. Kunsthistorisches Museum,
Vienna 528, 550. P. Vignon *The Shroud of Christ*, 1902,
546. Santa Marta de Terra, Zamora (Jean Dieuzaide)
542*l*.
Extracts from the New English Bible are reproduced
by permission of the Delegates of the Oxford
University Press and the Syndics of the Cambridge
University Press.

The Mandala

Prince of Wales Museum of Western India,
Bombay 580. Indian Museum, Calcutta 592.
Gerd-Wolfgang Essen 595, 596. Robert Fludd
Tomus Primus De Macrocosmi Historia, 1617, 579.
From the collection of Joan Halifax 573. Carl G.
Jung *Archetypes and the Collective Unconscious, Collected
Works*, 1959, 628, 629. Stanislaus Klossowski de Rola
620. Copyright British Museum, London 576, 591,
599. By courtesy of the Board of Trustees of the
Victoria & Albert Museum, London 560. Ajit
Mookerjee Collection 569, 570, 585, 586, 587, 588,
593, 604, 608, 612, 614, 616, 618, 619, 623, 625, 627.
Ronald Nameth 633. Musée Guimet, Paris 600.
Miranda Payne 630, 631. Private collection 561, 563,
565, 566, 575, 581, 582, 603, 610. Museum für
Völkerkunde, Zürich 606.
Extracts on the pages listed have come from the
following sources: *The Theory and Practice of the
Mandala*, Rider, 1961, © Giuseppe Tucci 571, 605, 607,
632; *The Upanishads*, Penguin, 1965, trans. © Juan
Mascaró 580, 622, 624, 626; *The Dhammapada*, Penguin,
1973, trans. © Juan Mascaró 587, 594, 598, 605, 609,
615; *Buddhist Scriptures*, Penguin, 1959, trans. © Edward
Conze 594, 597; *Speaking of Siva*, Penguin, 1973, trans.
© A. K. Ramanujan 583.